PICCADILLY

A FRAGMENT OF CONTEMPORARY BIOGRAPHY

BY

LAURENCE OLIPHANT

"Some make love in poetry, And some in—Piccadilly."

—PRAED.

"FAITHFUL.—'I say, then, in answer to what Mr Envy hath spoken, I never said aught but this, That what rule, or laws, or customs, or people, were flat against the Word of God, are diametrically opposed to Christianity. If I have said amiss in this, convince me of my error, and I am ready here, before you all, to make my recantation.'"—BUNYAN'S 'Pilgrim's Progress.'

PREFACE.

Five years have elapsed since the following pages were penned, and periodically issued, under an impulse which seemed at the time irresistible. I found myself unable, by any conscious act of volition, to control either the plot or the style. Nor from my present point of view do I particularly admire either the one or the other. At the same time, I have reason to hope that the republication of this sketch now, with all its defects, is calculated to do more good than harm to the society it attempts to delineate.

This conviction must be my apology for again forcing upon the public a fragment so hostile to it in tone and spirit. I would reiterate the observation made elsewhere in the work, that none of the characters are intended to represent any members of society who were then, or are now, alive.

PART I.

LOVE.

Piccadilly, *2d February 1865.*

In a window, a few doors from Cambridge House, the following placard some time since invited, apparently without much effect, the notice of the passers-by,—"To let, this desirable family mansion," After a considerable period the "desirable family" seem to have been given up in despair, and the words vanished from the scene; but the board in the window, beginning "to let" remained, while the "mansion" itself was converted upon it into "unfurnished chambers."

As, in the words of that "humble companion," whose life was rendered a burden to her by my poor dear mother, "Money was not so much an object as a comfortable home," I did not hesitate to instal myself in the first floor, which possessed the advantage of a bay-window, with a double sash to keep out the noise, together with an extensive view of Green Park, and a sailor without legs perpetually drawing ships upon the opposite pavement, as a foreground. My friend Lord Grandon, who is an Irish peer with a limited income, took the floor above, as I was desirous of securing myself against thumping overhead; moreover, I am extremely fond of him. When I say that the position which I enjoy socially, is as well adapted for seeing life as the locality I selected for my residence, most of my more fashionable readers will intuitively discover who I am; fortunately, I have no cause to desire to maintain an incognito which would be impossible, though, perhaps, I ought to explain the motives which induce me now to bring myself even more prominently before the public than I have been in the habit of doing.

Sitting in my bay-window the other evening, and reading the 'History of Civilisation,' by my late lamented friend Mr Buckle, it occurred to me that I also would write a history of civilisation—after having seen the world, instead of before doing so, as was the case with that gifted philosopher. Having for many years past devoted myself to the study of my fellow-men in all countries, I thought the time had come when I could, with profit to myself and the world, give it the benefit of my extended experience and my quick observation. No sooner had I arrived at this determination, than with characteristic promptitude I proceeded to put it into execution; and singular though it may appear, it was not until then that I found myself quite incompetent to carry out the vast project I had undertaken. The reason was at once apparent—I had seen and thought too much; and was in the position which my predecessor had failed to reach, of experimentally discovering that the task was beyond the human power of accomplishment. Not easily vanquished, I then thought of subdividing it, and dealing exclusively with a single branch of civilisation. Mr Thomas Taylor Meadows, thought I, has written a very elaborate chapter upon the progress of civilisation as regarded from a Chinese point of view, why should not I look upon it from a purely Piccadillean?—so I immediately looked at it. The hour 11 P.M.; a long string of carriages advancing under my windows to Lady Palmerston's; rain pelting; horses with ears pressed back, wincing under the storm; coachmen and footmen presenting the crowns of their hats to it; streams running down their waterproofs, and causing them to glitter in the gaslight; now and then the flash of a jewel inside the carriages; nothing visible of the occupants but flounces surging up at the windows, as if they were made of some delicious creamy substance, and were going to overflow into the street; policemen in large capes, and if I may be allowed the expression, "helmetically" sealed from the wet, keeping order; draggled women on foot "moving" rapidly on. The fine ladies in their carriages moving on too—but not quite so fast.

This Piccadillean view of the progress of civilisation suggested to me many serious reflections; among others, that if I intended to go to Cambridge House myself, the sooner I went to dress the better. Which way are we moving? I mused, as I made the smallest of white bows immediately over a pearl stud in my neck. I gave up the "history" of civilisation. I certainly can't call it "the progress" of civilisation; that does all very well for Pekin, not for London. Shall I do the Gibbon business, and call it "the decline and fall" of civilisation?—and I absently thrust two right-hand gloves into my pocket by mistake, and scrambling across the wet pavement into my brougham, drove in it the length of the file and arrived before I had settled this important question.

While Lady Veriphast, having planted me *en tête-à-tête* in a remote corner, was entertaining me with her accustomed vivacity, I am conscious of having gazed into those large swimming eyes with a vacant stare so utterly at variance with my usual animated expression, that she said at last, rather pettishly, "What *are* you thinking about?"

"Civilisation," I said, abruptly.

"You mean Conventionalism," she replied; "have you come to the conclusion, as I have, that all conventionalism is vanity?"

"No; only that it is 'vexation of spirit;' that is the part that belongs to us—we leave the 'vanity' to the women."

"Dear me, I never heard you so solemn and profound before. Are you in love?"

"No," I said; "I am thinking of writing a book, but I don't see my way to it."

"And the subject is the Conventionalism which you call civilisation. Well, I don't wonder at your looking vacant. You are not quite up to it, Lord Frank. Why don't you write a novel?"

"My imagination is too vivid, and would run away with me."

"Nothing else would," she said, laughing; "but if you don't like fiction, you can always fall back upon fact; be the hero of your own romance, publish your diary, and call it 'The Experiences of a Product of the Highest State of Civilisation.' Thus you will be able to write about civilisation and yourself at the same time, which I am sure you will like. I want some tea, please; do you know you are rather dull to-night?" And Lady Veriphast walked me into the middle of the crowd, and abandoned me abruptly for somebody else, with whom she returned to her corner, and I went and had tea by myself.

But Lady Veriphast had put me on the right track: why, I thought as I scrambled back again from my brougham across the wet pavement to my bay-window, should I not begin at once to write about the civilisation of the day? 'The Civilisation of the British Isles, as exhibited in Piccadilly, a Fragment of Contemporaneous Biography,' that would not be a bad title; people would think, if I called it a biography, it must be true; here I squared my elbows before a quantity of foolscap, dipped my pen in the ink, and dashed off the introduction as above.

Next morning I got up and began again as follows: Why should I commit the ridiculous error of supposing that the incidents of my daily life are not likely to interest the world at large? Whether I read the diary of Mr Pepys, or of Lady Morgan—whether I wade through the Journal of Mr Evelyn, or pleasantly while away an hour with the memoirs of "a Lady of Quality," I am equally struck with this traditional practice of the bores and the wits of society, to write at length the records of their daily life, bottle them carefully up in a series of MS. volumes, and leave them to their grandchildren to publish, and to posterity to criticise. Now it has always appeared to me that the whole fun of writing was to watch the immediate effect produced by one's own literary genius. If, in addition to this, it is possible to interest the public in the current events of one's life, what nobler object of ambition could a man propose to himself? Thus, though the circle of my personal acquaintances may not be increased, I shall feel my sympathies are becoming enlarged with each succeeding mark of confidence I bestow upon the numerous readers to whom I will recount the most intimate relations of my life. I will tell them of my aspirations and my failures—of my hopes and fears, of my friends and my enemies. I shall not shrink from alluding to the state of my affections; and if the still unfulfilled story of my life becomes involved with the destiny of others, and entangles itself in an inextricable manner, that is no concern of mine. I shall do nothing to be ashamed of, or that I can't tell; and if truth turn out stranger than fiction, so much the better for my readers. It may be that I shall become the hero of a sensation episode in real life, for the future looks vague and complicated enough; but it is much better to make the world my friend before anything serious occurs, than allow posterity to misjudge my conduct when I am no longer alive to explain it. Now, at least, I have the satisfaction of knowing that whatever happens I shall give my version of the story first. Should the daily tenor of my life be undisturbed, I can always fall back upon the exciting character of my opinions.

As I write, the magnitude of the task I propose to myself assumes still larger proportions. I yearn to develop in the world at large those organs of conscientiousness and benevolence which we all possess but so few exercise. I invoke the cooperation of my readers in this great work: I implore them to accompany me step by step in the crusade which I am about to preach in favour of the sacrifice of self for the public good. I demand their sympathy in this monthly record of my trials as an uncompromising exponent of the motives of the day, and I claim their tender solicitude should I writhe, crushed and mangled by the iron hand of a social tyranny dexterously concealed in its velvet glove. I will begin my efforts at reform with the Church; I may then possibly diverge to the Legislature, and I will mix in the highest circles of society in the spirit of a missionary. I will endeavour to show everybody up to everybody else in the spirit of love; and if they end by quarrelling with each other and with me, I shall at least have the satisfaction of feeling myself divested of all further responsibility in the matter. In my present frame of mind apathy would be culpable and weakness a crime....

Candour compels me to state that when, as I told Lady Veriphast, my imagination becomes heated, my pen travels with a velocity which fails to convey any adequate impression of the seething thoughts which course through my brain. I lose myself in my subject, and become almost insensible to external sensations; thus it happened that I did not hear the door open as I was writing the above, and I was totally unconscious as I was reading fervently aloud the last paragraph, containing those aspirations which I promised to confide to the public, that I had already a listener. Judge of my surprise—I may say dismay—when, just as I had finished, and was biting the end of my pen for a new inspiration, I heard the voice of Grandon close behind my chair. "Well done, my dear Frank," he said—and as he has known me from my boyhood, he can make allowances for my fervent nature. "Your programme is very complete, but I doubt your being able to carry it out. How, for instance, do you propose to open the campaign against the Church?"

If there is one quality upon which I pride myself more than another it is readiness. I certainly had not formed the slightest conception of how these burning thoughts of mine should be put into execution; but I did not hesitate a second in my answer. "I shall go down to a bishop and stay with him in his palace," I replied, promptly.

"Which one?" said Grandon.

I was going to say "Oxbridge," as he is the only one I happen to know; but, in the first place, I am a little afraid of him; and, in the second, I am hardly on sufficiently intimate terms with him to venture to propose myself—so I said, with some effrontery, "Oh, to a colonial bishop, whom you don't know."

"Nor you either, I suspect," laughed Grandon. "Just at present colonial bishops are rather scarce articles, and I have never heard of one in England with a palace, though there are a good many of them dotted about in snug livings, retaining only their lawn sleeves, either to laugh in or remind them of the dignity and the hardships of which they did not die abroad. Their temptations are of a totally different nature from theirs who are members of the House of Peers, and they must be treated apart; in fact, you will have to take them with the missionaries and colonial clergy. I quite agree with you that if there is one thing that is more urgently needed than a missionary to the ball-room, it is a missionary to the missionaries; and as you have had so much experience of their operations abroad, you might become a very useful labourer in the ecclesiastical vineyard."

I need scarcely say that my heart leaped at the thought; it was a work for which I felt myself specially qualified. "Why," I have thought, "should there be a set of men who preach to others, and are never preached at themselves? Every class and condition of life has its peculiar snares and temptations, and one class is set apart to point them out—surely there should be somebody to perform that kind office for them which they do for others. He who is paid to find out the mote that is in his brother's eye, and devotes his energies to its discovery, is of all men the one who requires the most kind and faithful friend to show him the beam which is in his own. I will be that friend, and charge nothing for it," thought I.

Grandon saw the flush of enthusiasm which mounted to my brow, and looked grave.

"My impulsive friend," he said, "this is a very serious subject; we must beware lest we fall into the error which we blame in others. It is one thing to see the need of the missionary, it is another to rush headlong upon the work. However, I am able to offer you an opportunity of beginning at once, for I have just come to tell you that Dickiefield has given us a joint invitation to go down to-morrow to Dickiefield, to stay till Parliament opens; we shall be certain to find a choice assortment of pagan and theological curiosities in that most agreeable of country-houses, and you may possibly meet the identical colonial bishop at whose palace you proposed staying. The three o'clock train lands us exactly in time for dinner. Will you come?"

"Of course I will. Nothing would justify my neglecting so promising a vineyard in which to commence my labours;" and I rubbed my hands enthusiastically, and sat down to write a series of those "consecrated lies" by means of which dinner engagements, already accepted, are at the last moment evaded.

DICKIEFIELD, *4th February.*

The party here consists of old Lady Broadhem, with that very aspiring young nobleman, her son, the young Earl (old Lord Broadhem died last year), and his sisters, Ladies Bridget and Ursula Newlyte, neither of whom I have seen since they emerged from the nursery.

They had all disappeared to dress for dinner, however, and Dickiefield had not come home from riding, so that when Grandon and I entered the drawing-room, we found only the deserted apparatus of the afternoon tea, a Bishop, and a black man—and we had to introduce ourselves. The Bishop had a beard and an apron, his companion a turban, and such very large shoes, that it was evident his feet were unused to the confinement. The Bishop looked stern and determined; perhaps there was just a dash of worldliness about the twist of his mustache. His companion wore a subdued and unctuous appearance; his face was shaved; and the whites of his eyes were very bloodshot and yellow. Neither of them was the least embarrassed when we were shown in; Grandon and I both were slightly. "What a comfort that the snow is gone," said I to the Bishop.

"Yes," said his lordship; "the weather is very trying to me, who have just arrived from the Caribbee Islands."

"I suppose you have accompanied his lordship from the Caribbee Islands," said I, turning to the swarthy individual, whom I naturally supposed to be a specimen convert.

"No," he said; "he had arrived some months since from Bombay."

"Think of staying long in England?" said Grandon.

"That depends upon my prospects at the next general election. I am looking out for a borough."

"Dear me!" said Grandon; and we all, Bishop included, gazed on him with astonishment.

"My name is Chundango," he went on. "My parents were both Hindoos. Before I was converted my other name was Juggonath; now I am John. I became acquainted with a circle of dear Christian friends in Bombay, during my connection, as catechist, with the Tabernacle Missionary Society, was peculiarly favoured in some mercantile transactions into which I subsequently entered in connection with cotton, and have come to spend my fortune, and enter public life, in this country. I was just expressing to our dear friend here," pointing in a patronising way towards the Bishop, "my regret at finding that he shares in views which are becoming so prevalent in the Church, and are likely to taint the Protestantism of Great Britain and part of Ireland."

"Goodness," thought I, "how this complicates matters! which of these two now stands most in need of my services as a missionary?" As Dickiefield was lighting me up to my bedroom, I could not resist congratulating him upon his two guests. "A good specimen of the 'unsound muscular,' the Bishop," said I.

"Not very," said Dickiefield; "he is not so unsound as he looks, and he is not unique, like the other. I flatter myself I have under my roof the only well-authenticated instance of the Hindoo converted millionaire. It is true he became a 'Government Christian' when he was a poor boy of fifteen, and began life as a catechist; then he saw a good mercantile opening, and went into cotton, out of which he has realised an immense fortune, and now is going into political life in England, which he could not have done in an unconverted condition. Who ever heard before of a Bombay man wanting to get into Parliament, and coming home with a *carte du pays* all arranged before he started? He advocates extension of the franchise, ballot, and the Evangelical Alliance, so I thought I would fasten him on to Broadhem—they'll help to float each other."

"Who else have you got here besides?" I asked.

"Oh, only a petroleum aristocrat from the oil regions of America—another millionaire. He is a more wonderful instance even than Chundango, for he was a poor man three months ago, when he 'struck oil.' You will find him most intelligent, full of information; but you will look upon him, of course, as the type of the peculiar class to which he belongs, and not of Americans generally." And my warm-hearted and eccentric friend, Lord Dickiefield, left me to my meditations and my toilet.

"I shall probably have to take one of these Broadhem girls in to dinner," thought I, as I followed the rustle of their crinolines down-stairs back to the drawing-room. So I ranged myself near the one with dark hair and blue eyes—I like the combination—to the great annoyance of Juggonath, who had got so near her for the same purpose that his great foot was on her dress.

"I beg your pardon, Mr Juggernaut," said I, giving him a slight shove, "I think you are standing——"

"Chundango, sir, if you please," said he, unconsciously making way for me, "Juggonath is the name which my poor benighted countrymen——"

"Juggernaut still speaking, as they say in the telegraphic reports from the House of Commons," I remarked to Lady Ursula, as I carried her off triumphantly; and the Indian's voice was lost in the hum of the general movement towards the dining-room.

I have promised not to shrink from alluding to those tender sensibilities which an ordinary mortal jealously preserves from the rough contact of his fellow-men; but I am not an ordinary mortal, and I have no hesitation in saying, that never in my life have I gone through such a distinct change of feeling in the same period as during the two hours we sat at that dinner. Deeply versed as I am in every variety of the sex, married or single, how was I to know that Lady Ursula was as little like the rest of the species as our Bombay friend was to wealthy Hindoos generally? What reason had I to suppose that Lady Broadhem's daughter could possibly be a new type?

Having been tolerably intimate at Broadhem House before she was out, I knew well the atmosphere which had surrounded her youth, and took it for granted that she had imbibed the family views.

"Interesting creature, John Chundango, Esq.," said I, for I thought she had looked grave at the flippancy of my last remark; "he has quite the appearance of a 'Brand.'"

"A what?" said Lady Ursula, as she looked up and caught him glaring fixedly at her with his great yellow eyeballs from the other side of the table.

"Of course I don't mean of the 'whipper-in' of the Liberal party, but of one rescued from fire. I understand that his great wealth, so far from having proved a snare to him, has enabled him to join in many companies for the improvement of Bombay, and that his theological views are quite unexceptionable."

"If his conversion leads him to avoid discussing either his neighbours or their theology, Lord Frank, I think he is a person whom we may all envy."

Is that a hit at her mother or at me? thought I. At Broadhem House, society and doctrine used to be the only topics of discussion. My fair friend here has probably had so much of it that she has gone off on another tack; perhaps she is a "still deep fast" one. As I thought thus, I ran over in my mind my young-lady categories, as follows:—

      {The wholly worldly
First,   {   and
      {The worldly holy.

In this case the distinction is very fine; but though they are bracketed together, there is an appreciable difference, which perhaps, some day when I have time, I shall discuss.

Second, "The still deep fast."

This may seem to be a contradiction in terms; but the fact is, while the upper surface seems tranquil enough, there is a strong rapid undercurrent. The danger is, in this case, that you are very apt to go in what is called a "header." The moment you dive you get caught by the undercurrent, and the chances are you never rise to the surface again.

Third, "The rippling glancing fast."

This is less fatal, but to my mind not so attractive as the other. The ripples are produced by quantities of pebbles, which are sure to give one what is called in America "a rough time." The glancing is only dangerous to youths in the first stage, and is perfectly innocuous after one season.

Fourth, "The rushing gushing fast."

This speaks for itself, and may be considered perfectly harmless.

There are only two slows—the "strong-minded blue slow," and the "heavy slow."

The "strong-minded blue slow" includes every branch of learning. It is extremely rare, and alarming to the youth of the day. I am rather partial to it myself.

The "heavy slow" is, alas! too common.

To return to Lady Ursula: not "worldly holy," that was quite clear; certainly neither of the "slows," I could see that in her eye, to say nothing of the retort; not "rippling glancing," her eye was not of that kind either; certainly not "rushing gushing." What remained? Only "Wholly worldly," or "still deep fast."

These were the thoughts that coursed through my mind as I pondered over her last remark. I had not forgotten that I had a great work to accomplish. The missionary spirit was ever burning within me, but it was necessary to examine the ground before attempting to prepare it for seed. I'll try her as "still deep," thought I.

"Did you go out much last season?" I said, by way of giving an easy turn to the conversation.

"No; we have been very little in London, but we are going up this year. We have always resisted leaving the country, but mamma wants to make a home for Broadhem."

"Ah! it is his first season, and naturally he will go out a great deal. Of course you know the three reasons which take men into society in London," I said, after a pause.

"No, I don't. What are they?"

"Either to find a wife, or to look after one's wife, or to look after somebody else's."

I was helping myself to potatoes as I made this observation in a tone of easy indifference; but as she did not immediately answer, I glanced at her, and was at once overcome with remorse and confusion; her neck and face were suffused with a glow which produced the immediate effect upon my sensitive nature of making me feel a brute; her very eyelids trembled as she kept them steadily lowered: and yet what had I said which I had not repeatedly said before to both the "slows," one of the "worldlies," and all the "fasts"? Even some of the "worldly holies" rather relish this style of conversation, though I always wait for them to begin it, for fear of accidents. Fortunately, however much I am moved, I never lose my presence of mind; so I deliberately upset my champagne-glass into her plate, and, with the delicacy and tact of a refined nature, so worded the apologies with, which I overwhelmed her, that she forgave my first *gaucherie* in laughing over the second.

She can be nothing now, thought I, but "wholly worldly," but she should be ticketed, like broadcloth, "superfine;" so I must tread cautiously.

"I hear Lord Broadhem is going to make his political *début* in a few days," I remarked, after a pause. "What line does he think of taking?"

"He has not told me exactly what he means to say, as I am afraid we do not quite agree in what philosophers call 'first principles,'" she replied, with a smile and a slight sigh.

"Ah!" I said, "I can guess what it is; he is a little too Radical for you, but you must not mind that; depend upon it, an ambitious young peer can't do better than ally himself with the Manchester school. They have plenty of talent, but have failed as yet to make much impression upon the country for lack of an aristocrat. It is like a bubble company in the City; they want a nobleman as chairman to give an air of respectability to the direction. He might perhaps be a prophet without honour if he remained in his own country, so he is quite right to go to Manchester. I look upon cotton, backed by Exeter Hall, as so strong a combination, that they would give an immense start in public life to a young man with great family prestige, even of small abilities; but as Broadhem has good natural talents, and is in the Upper House into the bargain, the move, in a strategical point of view, so far as his future career is concerned, is perfect."

"I cannot tell you, Lord Frank," said Lady Ursula, "how distressed I am to hear you talk in this way. As a woman, I suppose I am not competent to discuss politics; and if Broadhem conscientiously believes in manhood suffrage and the Low Church, and considers it his duty before God to lose no opportunity of propagating his opinions, I should be the first to urge his using all the influence which his name and wealth give him in what would then become a sacred duty; but the career that you talk about is not a sacred duty. It is a wretched Will-o'-the-wisp that tempts men to wade through mire in its pursuit, not the bright star fixed above them in the heavens to light up their path. I firmly believe," she went on, as she warmed to her theme, "that that one word 'Career,' has done more to demoralise public men than any other word in the language. It is one embodiment of that selfishness which we are taught from our cradles. Boys go to school with strict injunctions if possible to put self at the top of it. They take the highest honours at the university purely for the sake of self. How can we expect when they get into Parliament that they should think of anything but self, until at last the most conscientious of them is only conscientious by contrast? Who is there that ever tells them that personal ambition is a sin the most hateful in the sight of God, the *first* and not the last 'infirmity of noble minds'? I know you think me foolish and unpractical, and will tell me mine is an impossible standard; but I don't believe in impossible standards where public morality is concerned. At all events, let us make some attempt in an upward direction; and as a first step I propose to banish from the vocabulary that most pernicious of all words, 'A Career.'"

She stopped, with eyes sparkling and cheeks flushed; by the way, I did not before remark, for I only now discovered, that she was lovely—"wholly worldly"—what sacrilege! say rather "barely mortal;" and I forthwith instituted a new category. My own ideas, thought I, expressed in feminine language; she is converted already, and stands in no need of a missionary. Grandon himself could not take higher ground; as I thought of him I looked up, and found his eyes fixed upon us. "My friend Grandon would sympathise most cordially in your sentiments," I said, generously; for I had fallen a victim in preparing the ground; I had myself tumbled into the pit which I had dug for her; for had I not endeavoured to entrap her by expressing the most unworthy opinions, in the hope that by assenting to them she would have furnished me with a text to preach upon?

"Yes," she replied, in a low tone, and with a slight tremor in her voice, "I know what Lord Grandon's views are, for he was staying with us at Broadhem a few weeks ago, and I heard him upon several occasions discussing the subject with my brother."

"Failed to convert him, though, it would appear," said I, thinking what a delightful field for missionary operations Broadhem House would be. "Perhaps I should be more successful. Grandon wants tact. Young men sometimes require very delicate handling."

"So do young women," said Lady Ursula, laughing. "Will you please look under the table for my fan?" and away sailed the ladies, leaving me rather red from having got under the table, and very much in love indeed.

I was roused from the reverie into which I instantly fell by Dickiefield telling me to pass the wine, and asking me if I knew my next neighbour. I looked round and saw a young man with long flaxen hair, blue eyes, and an unhealthy complexion, dexterously impaling pieces of apple upon his knife, and conveying them with it to his mouth. "Mr Wog," said Dickiefield, "let me introduce you to Lord Frank Vanecourt."

"Who did you say, sir?" said Mr Wog, in a strong American accent, without taking the slightest notice of me.

"Lord Frank Vanecourt," said Dickiefield.

"Lord Frank Vanecourt, sir, how do you do, sir?—proud to make your acquaintance, sir," said Mr Wog.

"The same to you, sir," said I. "Pray, where were you raised?" I wanted to show Mr Wog that I was not such a barbarian as he might imagine, and knew how to ask a civil question or two.

"Well, sir, I'm a Missouri man," he replied. "I was a captain under Frank Blair, till I was taken bad with chills and fever; then I gave up the chills and kept the fever—'oil-fever' they call it down to Pithole—you've heard of Pithole?"

"Yes," I said, I had heard of that magical city.

"Well, just as I struck oil, one of your English lords came over there for the purpose of what he called 'getting up petroleum' and we were roommates in the same hotel for some time, and got quite friendly; and when he saw my new kerosene lamp, and found I was coming to have it patented in this country, he promised to help me to get up a Patent Lamp Company, and gave me letters to some of your leading aristocracy; so, before leaving, I saw the President, and told him I would report on the state of feeling in your highest circles about our war. We know what it is in your oppressed classes, but it aint every one has a chance, like me, of finding out how many copperheads there are among your lords. My father, sir, you may have heard of by name— Appollonius T. Wog, the founder, and, I may say, the father of the celebrated 'Pollywog Convention,' which was named after him, and which unfortunately burst up just in time to be too late to save our country from bursting up too."

I expressed to Mr Wog my condolences on the premature decease of the Pollywog Convention, and asked him how long he had been in England, and whom he had seen.

"Well, sir," he said, "I have only been here a few days, and I have seen considerable people; but none of them were noblemen, and they are the class I have to report upon. The Earl of Broadhem, here, is the first with whom I have conversed, and he informs me that he has just come from one of your universities, and that the sympathies of the great majority of your rising youth are entirely with the North."

"You may report to your Government that the British youth of the present day, hot from the university, are very often prigs."

"Most certainly I will," said Mr Wog; "the last word, however, is one with which I am not acquainted."

"It is an old English term for profound thinker," I replied.

Mr Wog took out a pocket-book, and made a note; while he was doing so, he said, with a sly look, "Have you an old English word for 'quite a fine gurl'?"

"No," I said; "they are a modern invention."

"Well, sir, I can tell you the one that sat 'twixt you and me at dinner would knock the spots out of some of our 'Sent' Louis belles."

In my then frame of mind the remark caused me such acute pain that I plunged into a conversation that was going on between Grandon and Dickiefield on the present state of our relations with Brazil, and took no further notice of Mr Wog for the rest of the evening; only, as my readers may possibly hear more of him in society during this season, I have thought it right to introduce him to them at once.

We all went to hear Broadhem's speech next day, and whatever might have been our private opinion upon the matter, we all, with the exception of Grandon and Lady Ursula, warmly congratulated him upon it afterwards. John Chundango and Joseph Caribbee Islands both made most effective speeches, but we did not feel the least called upon to congratulate them: they each alluded with great affection to the heathen and to Lord Broadhem. Chundango drew a facetious contrast between his lordship and an effeminate young Eastern prince, which was highly applauded by the audience that crowded the town-hall of Gullaby; and Joseph made a sort of grim joke about the probable effect of the "Court of Final Appeal" upon the theological tenets of the Caribbee Islanders, that made Lady Broadhem cough disapprobation, and everybody else on the platform feel uncomfortable. I confess I have rather a weakness for Joseph. He has a blunt off-hand way of treating the most sacred topics, that you only find among those who are professionally familiar with the subject. There is something refreshingly muscular in the way he lounges down to the smoking-room in an old grey shooting-coat, and lights the short black meerschaum, which he tells you kept off fever in the Caribbee Islands, while the smoke loses itself in the depths of his thick beard, which he is obliged to wear because of his delicate throat. There is a force and an ease in his mode of dealing with inspiration at such a moment which you feel must give him an immense ascendancy over the native mind.

He possesses what may be termed a dry ecclesiastical humour, differing entirely from Chundango's, whose theological fun takes rather the form of Scriptural riddles, picked up while he was a catechist. Neither he nor Broadhem smoke, so we had Wog and the Bishop to ourselves for half an hour before going to bed. "You must come and breakfast with me some morning in Piccadilly to meet my interesting friend Brother Chrysostom, my lord," said I.

I always like to give a bishop his title, particularly a missionary bishop; it is a point of ecclesiastical etiquette about which I have heard that the propagators of Christianity were very particular.

"If you will allow me, sir, I will join the party," said Mr Wog, before the Bishop could reply; "and as I don't know where Piccadilly is, I'll just ask the Bishop to bring me along. There is a good deal of law going on between your bishops just now," our American friend went on, "and I should like to know the rights of it. We in our country consider that your Ecclesiastical Court is a most remarkable institution for a Christian land. Why sir, law is strictly prohibited in a certain place; and it seems to me that you might as well talk of a good devil as a religious court. If it is wrong for a layman to go to law, it must be wrong for a bishop. What's sauce for the goose is sauce for the gander; that proverb holds good in your country as well as mine, don't it?"

"The Ecclesiastical Court is a court of discipline and doctrine rather than of law," said Dickiefield.

"Well, it's a court anyhow you fix it; and your parsons must be a bad lot to want a set of lawyers reg'larly trained to keep them in order."

"Perhaps Parson Brownlow would have been the better of a court of some kind," said the Bishop. "It seems to me that to be a minister of the Gospel at one moment, a colonel at another, and the Governor of a State at a third, illustrates the abuses which arise when such courts don't exist. With us, now, when a man once takes orders, he remains in them for the rest of his life."

"Even after he has concluded not to obey them, eh?" asked Mr Wog.

"Ah, Mr Wog," I interrupted, "before you return to the oil regions, you must make yourself acquainted with the enormous advantages connected with a State Church. You must grasp the idea that it is founded chiefly upon Acts of Parliament—that the clergy are only a paid branch of the Civil Service, exercising police functions of a very lofty and important character. The 'orders' come from the Queen, the 'Articles' are interpreted by the Privy Council, and 'England expects every clergyman to do his duty.' As I think some of the late doctrinal decisions of the judicial committee are questionable, I am drawing up a bill for the reform of the Protestant religion, and for the addition of a fortieth article to the existing thirty-nine. If I can carry it through both Houses of Parliament, all the convocations in Christendom cannot prevent the nation from accepting it as absolute divine truth; and I shall have the extreme satisfaction of feeling that I am manufacturing a creed for the masses, and thus securing a theological progress commensurate with our educational enlightenment. As long as the law of the land enables a majority of the Legislature to point out the straight and narrow way to the archbishops and bishops who have to lead their flocks along it, I have no fear for the future. It must be a comfort to feel, that if the worst comes to the worst, you have, as in the House of Commons, to lean upon 'my lord.'"

But the "dry ecclesiastical humour" of the Bishop, to which I have referred, did not evidently run in the same channel as mine.

"I don't think," he said, sternly, "that this is either the place or the mode in which to discuss subjects of so solemn a nature."

"I was only speaking of the system generally," I retorted, "and did not propose to enter here upon any doctrinal details of a really sacred character; those I leave to ecclesiastical dignitaries and learned divines with initials, to ventilate in a sweet Christian spirit in the columns of the daily press."

But the Bishop had already lit his candle, and with an abrupt "good night," vanished.

"Really, Frank," said Dickiefield, "it is not fair of you to drive my guests to bed before they have finished their pipes in that way. What you say may be perfectly true, but there can be no sort of advantage in stating it so broadly."

"My dear Dickiefield, how on earth is our friend Wog here to understand what his southern countryman would call 'our peculiar institution,' if somebody does not enlighten him? I want him, on his return, to point out to the President the advantage of substituting a State Church for the State rights which are so rapidly disappearing." Whereupon we diverged into American politics; and I asked Grandon an hour later, as we went to bed, what he thought of my first missionary effort.

"If the effect of your preaching is to drive your listeners away," he said, laughing, "I am afraid it will not meet with much success."

"It is a disagreeable task, but somebody must do it," I replied, feeling really discouraged. "It makes me quite sad to look at these poor wandering shepherds, who really mean to do right, but who are so utterly bewildered themselves, that they have lost all power of guiding their flocks without the assistance of lawyers. When did these latter bring back 'the key of knowledge,' that one of old said they had 'taken away?' or why are they not as 'blind leaders of the blind' now as they were then? If I speak harshly, it is because I fancy I see a ditch before them. I shall feel bound to trouble the Bishop again with a few practical remarks. There is no knowing whether even he may not be brought to perceive that you might as well try to extract warmth from an iceberg as divine inspiration from the State, and that a Church without inspiration is simply a grate without fire. The clergy may go on teaching for doctrine the commandments of men, and stand and shiver in a theology which comes to them filtered through the Privy Council, and which is as cold and gloomy as the cathedrals in which it is preached. But the congregations who are crying aloud for light and heat will go and look for them elsewhere."

"You are a curious compound, Frank," said Grandon; "I never knew a man whose moods changed so suddenly, or whose modes of thinking were so spasmodic and extreme; however, I suppose you are intended to be of some use in the world"—and he looked at me as a philosopher might at a mosquito.

"By the way, we must leave by the early train to-morrow if we want to get to town in time for the opening of Parliament."

"I think I shall stay over to-morrow," I answered. "Broadhem is going up, but the ladies are going to stay two days longer, and the House can open very well without me; besides, Chundango and the Bishop are going to stay over Sunday."

"That is an inducement, certainly," said Grandon. "Come, you must have some other reason!"

"My dear old fellow," said I, putting my hand on Grandon's shoulder, "my time is come at last. Haven't you remarked what low spirits I have been in since dinner? I can't bear it for another twenty-four hours! You know my impulsive sensitive nature. I must know my fate at once from her own lips."

"Whose own lips?" said Grandon, with his eyes very wide open.

"Lady Ursula's, of course!" I replied. "I knew her very well as a child, so there is nothing very sudden about it."

"Well, considering you have never seen her since, I don't quite agree with you," he said, in a deeper tone than usual. "In your own interest, wait till you know a little more of her."

"Not another day! Good-night!" and I turned from him abruptly.

"I'll put myself out of suspense to-morrow, and keep the public in it for a month," thought I, as I penned the above for their benefit, after which I indulged in two hours of troubled sleep.

PART II.

MADNESS.

F̲l̲i̲t̲y̲v̲i̲l̲l̲e̲, *March 20.*

As the event which I am about to recount forms the turning-point of my life—unless, indeed, something still more remarkable happens, which I do not at present foresee, to turn me back again—I do not feel that it would be either becoming, or indeed possible, for me to maintain that vein of easy cheerfulness which has characterised my composition hitherto. What is fun to you, O my reader! may be death to me; and nothing can be further from my intention than to excite the smallest tendency to risibility on your part at my misfortunes or trials. You will already have guessed what these are; but how to recur to those agonising details, how to present to you the picture of my misery in its true colours,—nothing but the stern determination to carry out my original design, and the conscientious conviction that "the story of my life from month to month" may be made a profitable study to my fellow-men, could induce me in this cold-blooded way to tear open the still unhealed wound.

I came down to breakfast rather late on the morning following the events narrated in the last chapter. Broadhem and Grandon had already vanished from the scene; so had Mr Wog, who went up to town to see what he called "the elephant,"—an American expression, signifying "to gain experience of the world." The phrase originated in an occurrence at a menagerie, and as upon this occasion Mr Wog applied it to the opening of Parliament, it was not altogether inappropriate. I found still lingering over the *debris* of breakfast my host and hostess, Lady Broadhem and her daughters, the Bishop and Chundango. The latter appeared to be having all the talk to himself, and, to give him his due, his conversation was generally entertaining.

"My dear mother," he was saying, "still unconverted, has buried all my jewellery in the back verandah. After I had cleared a million sterling, I divided it into two parts; with one part I bought jewels, of which my mother is an excellent judge, and the other I put out at interest. Not forgetting," with an upward glance, "a sum the interest of which I do not look for here."

"Then, did you give all your jewels to your mother?" asked Lady Broadhem.

"Oh no; she is only keeping them till I can bestow them upon the woman I choose for her daughter-in-law."

"Are you looking out for her now?" I asked, somewhat abruptly.

"Yes, my dear friend," said John; "I hope to find in England some Christian young person as a yoke-mate."

There was a self-satisfied roll of his eye as he said this, which took away from me all further desire for the bacon and eggs I had just put on my plate.

"Dear Mr Chundango," said Lady Broadhem, "tell us some of your adventures as a catechist in the Bombay Ghauts. Did you give up all when you became one? Was your family noble? and did you undergo much persecution from them?"

"The Rajah of Sattara is my first cousin," said Chundango, unblushingly; "but they repudiated me when I became a Christian, and deny the relationship."

"Are you going up to Convocation?" said Dickiefield to the Bishop, to divert attention from Chundango's last barefaced assertion. "I hear they are going to take some further action about the judgment on the 'Essays and Reviews.'"

"Yes," said Joseph; "and I see there is a chance of three new sees being created. I should like to talk over the matter with you. Considering how seriously my health has suffered in the tropics, and how religiously I have adhered to my Liberal opinions in politics even in the most trying climates, it might be worth while——"

"Excuse me for interrupting you, my dear lord," said Dickiefield, "but the present Government are not so particular about the political as the theological views of their bishops. When you remember that the Prime Minister of this country is held morally accountable for the orthodoxy of its religious tenets, you must at once perceive how essential it is, not only that he should be profoundly versed in points of Scriptural doctrine himself, but that he should never appoint a bishop of whose soundness he is not from personal knowledge thoroughly satisfied."

"I have no objection to talk over the more disputed points with him," said the Bishop. "When do you think he could spare a moment?"

"The best plan would be," replied Dickiefield, with a twinkle in his eye, "to catch him in the lobby of the House some evening when there is nothing particular going on. What books of reference would you require?"

The Bishop named one, when I interrupted him, for I felt Dickiefield had not put the case fairly as regarded the first Minister of the Crown.

"It is not the Premier's fault at all," said I; "he may be the most liberal theologian possible, but he has nothing to do with doctrine; that lies in the Chancellor's department. As the supreme arbiter in points of religious belief, and as the largest dispenser of spiritual patronage in the kingdom, it is evident that the qualifications for a Lord Chancellor should be not so much his knowledge of law, as his unblemished moral character and incapacity for perpetrating jobs. He is, in fact, the principal veterinary surgeon of the ecclesiastical stable, and any man in orders that he 'warrants sound' cannot be objected to on the score of orthodoxy. The Prime Minister is just in the same position as the head of any other department,—whoever passes the competitive examination he is bound to accept, but may use his own discretion as to promotion, and, of course, sticks to the traditions of the service. The fact is, if you go into the Colonial Episcopal line you get over the heads of a lot of men who are steadily plodding on for home promotion, and, of course they don't think it fair for an outsider to come back again, and cut them out of a palace and the patronage attached to it on the strength of having been a missionary bishop. It is just the same in the Foreign Office,—if you go out of Europe you get out of the regular line. However, we shall have the judgment on the Colenso case before long, and, from the little I know of the question, it is possible you may find that you are not legally a bishop at all. In that case you will have what is far better than any interest—a grievance. You can say that you were tempted to give up a good living to go to the heathen on false pretences, and they'll have to make it up to you. You could not do better than apply for one of the appointments attached to some cathedrals, called 'Peculiars.' I believe that they are very comfortable and independent. If you will allow me I will write to my solicitor about one. Lawyers are the men to manage these matters, as they are all in with each other, and every bishop has one attached to him."

"Thank you, my lord—my observation was addressed to Lord Dickiefield," said the Bishop, very stiffly; for there was an absence of that deference in my tone to which those who love the uppermost seats in the synagogues are accustomed, but which I reserve for some poor labourers who will never be heard of in this world.

"Talking of committees," I went on, "how confused the Lord Chancellor must be between them all. He must be very apt to forget when he is 'sitting' and when he is being 'sat upon.' If he had not the clearest possible head, he would be proving to the world that Mr E⸻ was competent to teach the Zulus theology in spite of the Bishop of Cape Town, and that he was justified in giving Dr Colenso a large retiring pension. What with having to quote texts in one committee-room, and arithmetic in another, and having to explain the law of God, the law of the land, and his own conduct alternately, it is a miracle that he does not get a softening of the brain. Depend upon it," said I, turning to the Bishop, who looked flushed and angry, "that a 'Peculiar' is a much snugger place than the Woolsack."

"Lord Frank, permit me to say," broke in Lady Broadhem, who had several times vainly endeavoured to interrupt me, "that your manner of treating sacred subjects is most disrespectful and irreverent, and that your allusions to an ecclesiastical stable, 'outsiders,' and other racing slang, is in the worst possible taste, considering the presence of the Bishop."

"Lady Broadhem," said I, sternly, "when the money-changers were scourged out of the Temple there was no want of reverence displayed towards the service to which it was dedicated; and it seems to me, that to sell 'the Temple' itself, whether under the name of an 'advowson,' a 'living,' or a 'cure of souls,' is the very climax of irreverence, not to use a stronger term; and when the Lord Chancellor brings in an Act for the purpose of facilitating this traffic in 'souls,' and 'augmenting the benefices' derived from curing them, I think it is high time, at the risk of giving offence to my friend the Bishop, and to the ecclesiastical establishment generally, to speak out. What times have we fallen upon that the priesthood itself, once an inspiration, has become a trade?"[1]

Lady Broadhem seemed a little cowed by my vehemence, which some might have thought amounted to rudeness, but would not abandon the field. "The result," she said, "of impoverishing the Church will be, that you will only get literates to go into it; as it is, compared with other professions, it holds out no inducement for young men of family. Fortunately our own living, being worth £1200 a-year, always secures us a member of the family, and therefore a gentleman; but if you did away with them you would not have holier men, but simply worse-bred ones. I am sure we should not gain by having the Church filled with clergy of the class of Dissenting preachers."

"I don't think you would, any more than the Pharisees would have gained by being reduced to the level of the Sadducees; not that I would wish to use either term offensively towards the conscientious individuals who were, doubtless, comprised in the above sects in old time, still less as a reproach to the excellent men who fill the churches and chapels of this country now; but it has possibly not occurred to them that the Churchianity of the present day bears as little resemblance to the Christianity of eighteen hundred years ago, as the latter did to the worship it came to supersede;" and I felt I had sown seed in the ecclesiastical vineyard, and would leave it to fructify. "Good fellow, Frank!" I overheard Dickiefield say, as I left the room; "it is a pity his head is a little turned!" "Ah," I thought, "something is upside down; perhaps it is my head, but I rather think it is the world generally, including always the religious world. It seemed to have taken a start in the right direction nearly two thousand years ago, and now it has all slipped back again worse than ever, and is whirling the wrong way with a rapidity that makes one giddy. I feel more giddy than usual to-day, somehow," I soliloquised; "and every time I look at Lady Ursula, I feel exactly as if I had smoked too much. It can't be really that, so I'll light a cigar and steady my nerves before I come to the tremendous issue. She is too sensible to mind my smelling of tobacco." These were the thoughts that passed through my somewhat bewildered brain, as I stepped out upon the terrace and lit my cigar. So far from my nerves becoming steadier, however, under the usually soothing influence, I felt my heart beating more rapidly each time I endeavoured to frame the sentence upon which was to depend the happiness of my life, until at last my resolution gave way altogether, and I determined to put upon paper, in the form of an interrogatory, the momentous question. A glass door opened from a recess in the drawing-room upon the terrace on which I was walking, and in it, on my former visits, I had been in the daily habit of writing my letters. It was a snug retreat, with a fire all to itself, a charming view, and a *portière* which separated it or not from the drawing-room, according to the wish of the occupant. The first question I had to consider when I put the writing materials before me was, whether I ought to begin, "Dear Lady Ursula," or, "My dear Lady Ursula." I should not have entertained the idea of beginning "My dear," did I not feel that having known her as a child entitled me to assume a certain intimacy. However, on further consideration, I adopted the more distant form, and then my real difficulty began. While looking for an inspiration at the further end of the avenue which stretched from the lawn, I became conscious of a figure moving slowly towards me, which I finally perceived to be that of Lady Broadhem herself. In my then frame of mind, any escape from my dilemma was a relief, and I instinctively left the still unwritten note and joined her.

"This is a courageous proceeding, Lady Broadhem; the weather is scarcely mild enough for strolling."

"I determined to make sure of some exercise," she replied,—"the clouds look threatening; besides, I have a good deal on my mind, and I can always think better when I am walking *alone*."

She put a marked emphasis on the last word, I can't imagine why, so I said, "That is just my case. If you only knew the torture I am enduring, you would not wonder at my wanting to be alone. As for exercise, it would not be of the slightest use."

"Dear me," said Lady Broadhem, pulling a little box like a card-case out of her pocket, "tell me your exact symptoms, and I'll give you some globules."

"It is not altogether beyond the power of homœopathy," I said, with a sigh. "Hahnemann was quite right when he adopted as the motto for his system, 'Like cures like,' It applies to my complaint exactly. Love will cure love, but not in homœopathic doses."

"How very odd! I was thinking the very same thing when you joined me. My dear girls are of course ever uppermost in my mind, and I really am troubled about Ursula. I think," she said, looking with a sidelong glance into my face, "I know who is on the point of declaring himself," and she stopped suddenly, as though she had spoken under some irresistible impulse.

I don't remember having blushed since I first went to school, but if Lady Broadhem could have seen the colour of my skin under my thick beard, she would have perceived how just her penetration had been. Still I was a good deal puzzled at the quickness with which she had made a discovery I imagined unknown, even to the object of my affections, to say nothing of the coarseness of her alluding to it to me in that direct manner. What had I said or done that could have put her on the scent? I pondered in vain over the mystery. My conduct had been most circumspect during the few hours I had been in love; nothing but the sagacity with which the maternal instinct is endowed could account for it.

"Do you think Lady Ursula returns the affection?" said I, timidly.

"Ursula is a dear, well-principled girl, who will make any man who is fortunate enough to win her happy. I am sure she will be guided by my wishes in the matter. And now, Lord Frank, I think we have discussed this subject sufficiently. I have said more, perhaps, than I ought; but we are such old friends that, although I entirely disagree with your religious opinions, it has been a relief to me even to say thus much. I trust my anxieties will soon be at an end;" with which most encouraging speech Lady Broadhem turned towards the house, leaving me overcome with rapture and astonishment, slightly tinged with disgust at finding that the girl I loved was thrown at my head.

I did not delay, when I got back to my recess in the drawing-room, to tear up with a triumphant gesture my note beginning "Dear," and to commence another, "My dear Lady Ursula."

"The conversation which I have just had with Lady Broadhem," I went on, "encourages me to lose no time in writing to you to explain the nature of those feelings which she seems to have detected almost as soon as they were called into existence, and which gather strength with such rapidity that a sentiment akin to self-preservation urges me not to lose another moment in placing myself and my fortune at your disposal. If I allude to the latter, it is not because I think such a consideration would influence you in the smallest degree, but because you may not suspect, from my economical habits, the extent of my private resources. I am well aware that my impulsive nature has led me into an apparent precipitancy in writing thus; but if I cannot flatter myself that the short time I have passed in your society has sufficed to inspire you with a reciprocal sentiment, Lady Broadhem's assurance that I may depend upon your acceding to her wishes in this the most important act of your life, affords me the strongest encouragement.—Believe me, yours most faithfully,

"FRANK VANECOURT."

I have already observed that, when my mind is very deeply absorbed in composition, I become almost insensible to external influences: thus it was not until I had finished my letter, and was reading it over, that I became conscious of sounds in the drawing-room. I was just thinking that I had got the word "sentiment" twice, and was wondering what I could substitute for that expressive term, when I suppose I must have overheard, for I insensibly found myself signing my name "Jewel." Then came the unmistakable sound of Chundango's voice mentioning the name dearest to me. "Remember, Lady Ursula," said that regenerate pagan, "there are very few men who could offer their brides such a collection of jewels as I can. Think, that although of a different complexion from yourself, I am of royal blood. You are surely too enlightened and noble-minded to allow the trivial consideration of colour to influence you."

"Mr Chundango," said Lady Ursula, and I heard the rustle of her dress as she rose from her chair, "you really must excuse me from listening to you any more."

"Stop one moment," said Chundango; and I suspect he tried to get hold of her hand, for I heard a short quick movement; "I have not made this proposal without receiving first the sanction of Lady Broadhem." "Deceitful old hypocrite"; thought I, with suppressed fury. "When I told her ladyship that I would settle a million's worth of pounds upon you in jewellery and stock, that my blood was royal, and that all my aspirations were for social distinction, she said she desired no higher qualification. 'What, dear Mr Chundango,' she remarked, 'matters the colour of your skin if your blood is pure? If your jewellery and your conversion are both genuine, what more could an anxious mother desire for her beloved daughter?'"

"Spare me, I implore you," said Ursula, in a voice betraying great agitation. "You don't know the pain you are giving me."

Whether Chundango at this moment fell on his knees, which I don't think likely, as natives never thus far humble themselves before the sex, or whether he stumbled over a footstool in trying to prevent her leaving the room—which is more probable—I could not discover. I merely heard a heavy sound and then the door open. I think the Indian must have hurt himself, as the next time I heard his voice it was trembling with passion.

"Lady Broadhem," he said—for it appears she it was who had entered the room—"I do not understand Lady Ursula's conduct. I thought obedience to parents was one of the first precepts of the Christian religion; but when I tell her your wishes on the subject of our marriage, she forbids me to speak. I will now leave her in your hands, and I hope I shall receive her from them in the evening in another and a better frame of mind;" and Chundango marched solemnly out and banged the door after him.

"What have you done, Ursula?" said Lady Broadhem, in a cold, hard voice. "I suppose some absurd prejudice about his colour has influenced you in refusing a fortune that few girls have placed at their feet. He is a man of remarkable ability; in some lights there is a decided richness in his hue; and Lord Dickiefield tells me he fully expects to see him some day Under-Secretary for India, and ultimately perhaps in the Cabinet. Moreover, he is very lavish, and would take a pride in giving you all you could possibly want, and in meeting all our wishes. He would be most useful to Broadhem, whose property, you know, was dreadfully involved by his father in his young days-in fact, he promised me to pay off £300,000 of the debt upon his personal security, and not ask for any interest for the first few years. All this you are throwing away for some girlish fancy for some one else."

Here my heart bounded. "Dear girl," thought I, "she loves me, and I'll rush in and tell her that I return her passion. Moreover, I will overwhelm that old woman with confusion for having so grossly deceived me." A scarcely audible sob from Lady Ursula decided me, and to the astonishment of mother and daughter I suddenly revealed myself. Lady Ursula gave a start and a little exclamation, and before I could explain myself, had hurried from the room. Lady Broadhem confronted me, stern, defiant, and indignant.

"Is it righteous,—Lady Broadhem———" I began, but she interrupted me.

"My indignation? Yes, Lord Frank, it is."

"No, Lady Broadhem; I did not allude to your indignation, which is unjustifiable. I was about to express my feelings in language which I thought might influence you with reference to the deception you have practised upon me. You gave me to understand only half an hour ago that you approved of my attachment to your daughter; you implied that that attachment was returned—indeed, I have just overheard as much from her own lips; and now you deliberately urge her to ally herself with—the thought is too horrible!" and I lifted my handkerchief to my eyes to conceal my unaffected emotion.

"Lord Frank," said Lady Broadhem, calmly, "you had no business to overhear anything; however, I suppose the state of your feelings must be your excuse. It seems that we entirely misunderstood each other this morning. The attachment I then alluded to was the one you have just heard Mr Chundango declare. I did so, because I thought of asking you to find out some particulars about him which I am anxious to know. I was utterly ignorant of your having entertained the same feelings for Ursula. What settlements are you prepared to make?"

This question was put so abruptly that a mixed feeling of indignation and contempt completely mastered me. At these moments I possess the faculty of sublime impertinence.

"I shall make Broadhem a liberal allowance, and settle an annuity upon yourself, which my solicitor will pay you quarterly. I know the family is poor; it will give me great pleasure to keep you all."

Lady Broadhem's lips quivered with anger; but the Duke of Dunderhead's second son, who had inherited all the Flityville property through his mother, was a fish worth landing, so she controlled her feelings with an effort of self-possession which commanded my highest admiration, and said in a gentle tone as she held out her hand with a subdued smile,—

"Forgive the natural anxiety of a mother, Lord Frank, as I forgive you for that last speech." Here she lifted her eyes and remained silent for a few moments, then she sighed deeply. She meant me to understand by this that she had been permitted to overcome her feelings of resentment towards me, and was now overflowing with Christian charity.

"Dear Lady Broadhem," I replied, affectionately, for I felt preternaturally intelligent, and ready for the most elaborate maternal strategy, "how thankful we ought to be that on an occasion of this kind we can both so thoroughly command our feelings! Believe me, your anxiety for your daughter's welfare is only equalled by the fervour of my affection for her. Shall we say £100,000 in stock, and Flityville Park as a dower-house?"

"What stock, Lord Frank?" asked her ladyship, as she subsided languidly into a chair; "not Mexicans or Spanish passives, I do most fervently trust."

"No," said I, maliciously; "nearly all in Confederate and Greek loans."

"Oh!" she ejaculated, with a little scream, as if something had stung her.

"What is the matter, Lady Broadhem?" and she looked so unhappy and disconcerted that I had compassion on her. "I was only joking; you need be under no apprehension as to the securities—they are as sound as your own theology, and would satisfy the Lord Chancellor quite as well."

"Oh, it was not that! Perhaps some day when you and dear Ursula are married, I will tell you all about it; for you have my full consent; and I need not say what an escape I think she has had from that black man. *Entre nous*, as it is most important you should understand exactly the situation, I must correct one error into which you have fallen; she is not in love with you, Lord Frank; you must expect a little opposition at first; but that will only add zest to the pursuit, and my wishes will be paramount in the end. The fact is, but this is a profound secret, your friend Lord Grandon has behaved most improperly in the matter. He came down on some pretence of instilling his ridiculous notions into Broadhem, who took a fancy to him when we were all staying at Lady Mundane's, and I strongly opposed it, as I fancied, even then, he was paying Ursula too much attention; but she has such influence with Broadhem that she carried her point, because, she said, her brother could only get good from him. What exactly passed at Broadhem I don't know; but I was so angry at the idea of an almost penniless Irish peer taking advantage of his opportunities as a visitor to entrap my girl's affections, that I told him I expected some people, and should want his bedroom. He left within an hour, and Ursula declares he never uttered a word which warranted this decisive measure; but people can do a good deal without 'uttering,' as she calls it; and I am quite determined not to let them see anything of each other during the season. Fortunately Lord Grandon scarcely ever goes out, and Broadhem, whose eyes are opened at last, has promised to watch him. Whoever Ursula marries must do something for Broadhem."

Although I am able to record this speech word for word, I am quite unable to account for the curious psychological fact, that it has become engraven on my memory, while, at the time, I was unconscious of listening to it. The pattern of the carpet, a particular curl of Lady Broadhem's "front," the fact that the clock struck one, are all stamped upon the plate of my internal perceptive faculties with the vividness of a photograph. The vision of happiness which I had conjured up was changing into a hideous contrast, and reminded me of the Diorama at the Colosseum in my youth, where a fairy landscape, with a pastoral group at lunch in the foreground, became gradually converted into a pandemonium of flames and devils.

I felt borne along by a mighty torrent which was sweeping me from elysian fields into some fathomless abyss. Love and friendship both coming down together in one mighty crash, and the only thing left standing—Lady Broadhem—right in front of me—a very stern reality indeed. I don't the least know the length of time which elapsed between the end of her speech and when I returned to consciousness—probably not many seconds, though it seemed an age. I gasped for breath, so she kindly came to my relief.

"My dear Lord Frank," she said, "after all it might have been worse. Supposing that Lord Grandon had not been your friend, or had not had the absurd Quixotic ideas which I understand he has of the duties of friendship, he might have given you immense trouble; as it is, I am sure he has only to know the exact state of the case to retire. I know him quite well enough for that. I look upon it as providential. Had it been Mr Chundango, Grandon would most probably have persevered. Now he is quite capable of doing all he can to help you with Ursula."

I groaned in spirit. How well had Lady Broadhem judged the character of the man to whom she would not give her daughter!

"I am so glad to think, Lady Broadhem," said I, with a bitter laugh, "that you do not suspect me of such a ridiculous exaggeration of sentiment. So far from it, it seems to impart a peculiar piquancy to the pursuit when success is only possible at the sacrifice of another's happiness; and when that other is one's oldest friend, there is a refinement of emotion, a sort of pleasurable pain, which is quite irresistible. To what element in our nature do you attribute this?"

"To original sin, I am afraid," said Lady Broadhem, looking down, for my manner seemed to puzzle, and make her nervous.

"Oh, it is not at all 'original,'" said I. "Whatever other merit it possesses, it can't claim originality—it is the commonest thing in the world; but I think it is an acquired taste at first—it grows upon you like caviar or olives. I remember some years ago, in Australia, running away with the wife of a charming fellow——"

"Oh, Lord Frank, Lord Frank, please stop! Have you repented? and where is she?"

"No," I said, "I never intend to repent; and I'll tell you where she is after the marriage."

At this crisis the demon of recklessness which had sustained me, and prompted the above atrocious falsehood, deserted me suddenly, so I leant against the mantelpiece and sobbed aloud. I remember deriving a malicious satisfaction from the idea that Lady Broadhem thought I was weeping for my imaginary Australian.

"How very dreadful!" said she, when I became somewhat calmer. "We must forget the past, and try and reform ourselves, mustn't we?" she went on, caressingly; "but I had no idea that you had passed through a *jeunesse orageuse*. Do you know, I think men, when they do steady, are always the better for it."

"Well, I hope Lady Ursula may keep me quiet; nothing else ever has yet. I suppose you won't expect me to go to church?"

"We'll talk about that after the marriage, to use your own expression," replied Lady Broadhem, with a smile.

"Because, you know, I am worse than Grandon as regards orthodoxy. Now, Chundango is so thoroughly sound, don't you think, after all, that that is the first consideration?"

"To tell you the truth—but of course I never breathed it to Ursula—I attach a good deal of importance to colour."

"Ah, I see; you classify us somewhat in this way: first, if you can get it, rich, orthodox, and white; second, rich, heterdox, and white; third, rich, orthodox, and black. Now, in my opinion, to attach any importance whatever to colour is wicked. My objections to Mr Chundango do not apply to his skin, which is as good as any other, but to his heart, which I am afraid is black. I prefer a pure heart in a dark skin to a black heart in a white one," and I looked significantly at her ladyship. "Supposing that out of friendship for Grandon I should do the absurd thing of withdrawing my pretensions, what would happen?"

"I should insist upon Ursula's marrying Mr Chundango. I tell you in confidence, Lord Frank, that pecuniary reasons, which I will explain more fully at another time, render it absolutely necessary that she should marry a man with means within the next six months. The credit of our whole family is at stake; but it is impossible for me to enter into details now." At this moment the luncheon was announced. I followed Lady Broadhem mechanically towards the dining-room, but instead of entering it went up-stairs like one in a dream, and ordered my servant to make arrangements for my immediate departure. I pulled an arm-chair near my bedroom fire, and gazed hopelessly into it.

People call me odd. I wonder really whether the conflicts of which my brain is the occasional arena are fiercer than those of others. I wonder whether other people's thoughts are as like clouds as mine are—sometimes, when it is stormy, grouping themselves in wild fantastic forms; sometimes chasing each other through vacancy, for no apparent purpose; sometimes melting away in "intense inane;" and again consolidating themselves, black and lowering, till they burst in a passionate explosion. What are they doing now? and I tried in vain to stop the mental kaleidoscope which shifted itself so rapidly that I could not catch one combination of thought before it was succeeded by another; but always the same prominent figures dodging madly about the chambers of my brain—Chundango, Ursula, Lady Broadhem, and Grandon; Lady Broadhem, Chundango, Grandon, and Ursula—backwards and forwards, forwards and backwards, like some horrid word that I had to spell in a game of letters, and could never bring right. Love, friendship, hate, pity, admiration, treachery—more words to spell, ever combining wrongly, and never letting me rest, till I thought something must crack under the strain. Then mockingly came a voice ringing in my ears—Peace, peace, peace—and I fancied myself lulled to rest in her arms, and I heard the cooing of doves mingle with the soft murmur of her voice as she leant wistfully over me, and I revelled in that most fatal of all nightmares—the nightmare of those who, perishing of hunger and thirst, die of imaginary banquets. "Sweet illusion," I said, "dear to me as reality, brood over my troubled spirit, deaden its pain, heal its wounds, and weave around my being this delicious spell for ever." Then suddenly, as though my brain had been a magazine into which a spark had fallen, it blazed up; my hair bristled, and drops stood upon my forehead, for a great fear had fallen upon me. It had invaded me with the force of an overwhelming torrent, carrying all before it. It said, "Whence is the calm that soothes you? Infatuated dreamer, think you it is the subsiding of the storm, and not rather the lull that precedes it? Beware of the sleep of the frozen, from which there is no waking." What was this? was my mind regaining its balance, or was it going to lose it for ever? Most horrid doubt! the very thought was so much in the scale on the wrong side. Oh for something to lean upon—some strong stay of common-sense to support me! I yearned for the practical—some fact on which to build. "I have got it," I exclaimed suddenly. "There must be some osseous matter behind my dura mater!" I shall never forget the consolation which this notion gave me: it relieved me from any further psychological responsibility, so to speak; I gave up mental analysis. I attributed the keen susceptibility of my æsthetic nature to this cause, and accepted it as I would the gout, without a murmur. Still I needed repose and solitude, so I determined to go to Flityville and arrange my ideas, no longer alarmed at the confusion in which they were, but with the steadfast purpose of disentangling them quietly, as I would an interesting knot. Hitherto I had been tearing at it madly and making it worse; now I had got the end of the skein—"osseous matter"—and would soon unravel it. So I descended calmly to the drawing-room.

I found it empty, but it occurred to me I had left my letter to Lady Ursula in the recess, and in the agitation attending my interview with Lady Broadhem, had forgotten to go back for it. I pushed back the *portière*, and saw seated at the writing-table Lady Ursula herself. She looked pale and nervous, while I felt overwhelmed with confusion and embarrassment. This was the more trying, as many years have elapsed since I have experienced any such sensations.

"Oh, you don't happen to have seen a letter lying about anywhere, do you, Lady Ursula?" said I. "It ought to be under your hand, for I left it exactly on that spot."

"No," she said; "I found mamma writing here when I came, and she took a packet of letters away with her; perhaps she put yours among them by mistake. She will be back from her drive almost immediately."

"I hope so," said I. "I should be sorry to leave without seeing her."

"To leave, Lord Frank! I thought you were going to stay till Monday." She looked up rather appealingly, I thought, as if my presence would have been a satisfaction to her under the circumstances; and I saw, as I returned her steady earnest gaze, that she little guessed the purport of the missing letter.

At that moment my head began to swim, and the figures to dance about in my brain again. Chundango and Grandon seemed locked in a death-struggle, and Ursula, with dishevelled hair, trying to separate them, while Lady Broadhem, in the background, was clapping her hands and urging them on. I seemed spinning round the group with such rapidity that I was obliged to steady myself with one hand against the back of Lady Ursula's chair.

"What's the matter? what's the matter, Lord Frank?" she exclaimed.

"Osseous matter, osseous matter," I murmured mechanically, and it sounded so like an echo of her words that I am sure she thought me going mad. Should I throw myself at her feet and tell her all? If she would only trample upon me and my feelings together, it would be a luxury compared to the agony of self-control I was inflicting upon myself. If I could only pour myself out in a torrent of passionate expression, and wind up with a paroxysm of tears, she was welcome to treat me as a raving lunatic, but I should be much less likely to become one. But how, knowing what I did, could I face Grandon afterwards? Before that fatal conversation with Lady Broadhem, I should have had the satisfaction of hearing my fate from Lady Ursula herself, and I know that she would have treated me so tenderly that rejection would have been a thousand times preferable to this. She would have known then the intensity of my affection, she would have heard from my own lips the burning words with which I would have pleaded my cause, and, whatever might have been the result, would have pitied and felt for me. Now, if I say nothing, and Lady Broadhem tells her when I am gone that she considers us engaged, what will Ursula think of me? Again, if Lady Broadhem thinks I am really going to do what my conscience urges, and sacrifice myself for Grandon, then, poor girl, she will be sacrificed to Chundango.

Nothing but misery will come out of that double event: if I do what is right, it will bring misery; if I do what is wrong, it will bring misery too,—that is one consolation—it makes the straight and narrow path easier. The only difficulty is, I can't find it—and standing here with my hand on her chair, my head swimming, and Lady Ursula looking anxiously up at me, I am not likely to find it.

"Lord Frank, do let me ring the bell and send for a glass of water," she said at last.

"Thanks, no; the fact is, that letter I have lost causes me the greatest anxiety, and when I thought what the consequences might be of its going astray I felt a little faint for a moment."

"Dear me," said Lady Ursula, kindly, "I will make mamma look for it at once, and I am sure if it is a matter in which my sympathy could be of any use, you will appreciate my motive in offering it; but I do think in this world people might be of so much more use to each other than they are, if they would only trust one another, and believe in the sincerity of friendship. Although you did try to shock me last night," she said, with a smile, "I have heard so much of you from Lord Grandon, and know how kind and good you are, although he says you are too enthusiastic and too fond of paradoxes, but I assure you I consider you quite an old friend. You remember, years ago, when I was a little girl, how you used to gallop about with me on my pony in the park at Broadhem? You won't think me inquisitive, I am sure, in saying this, but there are moments sometimes when it is a relief to find a listener to the history of one's troubles."

"But when, by a curious fatality, that listener is the cause of them all, these moments are not likely to arrive," I thought, but did not say. Is it not enough to love a woman to distraction, and be obliged by every principle of honour to conceal it from her, without her pressing upon you her sympathy, and inviting your confidence? and the very tenderness which had prompted her speech rose up against her in judgment in my mind. So ready with her friendship, too! Should I tell her bitterly that she was the only being in the whole world whose friendship could aggravate my misery? Should I congratulate her upon the ingenuity she had displayed in thus torturing me? or should I revenge myself by giving her the confidence she asked, and requesting her to advise me how to act under the circumstances? Then I looked at the gentle earnest face, and my heart melted. My troubles! Do I not know too well what hers are? Perhaps it would be a relief to her to hear, that if worse comes to worst, she can always escape Chundango by falling back upon me. If she is driven to begging me to offer myself up on her shrine, what a very willing sacrifice she would find me! As she knows that I must have overheard what passed between her and Chundango this morning, shall I make a counter-proposition of mutual confidence, and allude delicately to that most painful episode! If she is generous enough to forget her own troubles and think of me, why should not I forget mine and think of her? The idea of this contradiction in terms struck me as so exquisitely ludicrous, that I laughed aloud.

"Ha! ha! ha! Lady Ursula, if you only knew what a comic aspect that last kind speech of yours has given to the whole affair. Don't think me ungrateful or rude, but—ha! ha! ha!" Here I went off again. "When once my sense of humour is really touched, I always seem to see the point of a joke to quite a painful degree. Upon two occasions I have suffered from fits after punning, and riddles always make me hysterical; but I assure you, you unconsciously made a joke just now when you asked me to tell you exactly what I felt, which I shall remember as long as I live, for it will certainly be the death of me—ha! ha! ha!" But Lady Ursula had risen from her chair and rung the bell before I had finished my speech, and I was still laughing when the servant came into the room, followed by Lady Broadhem and Lady Bridget.

"Dear me," said Lady Broadhem, with her most winning smile, "how very merry you are!—at least Lord Frank is. You seem a little pale, dear," turning to Ursula; "what is the matter?"

"Oh, nothing, mamma. Lord Frank has been looking for a letter in the recess. You don't happen to have put it up with yours, do you?"

"No, my dear, I think not," said Lady Broadhem, looking through a bundle. "Who was it to, Lord Frank, if you will pardon my curiosity? I shall find it more easily if you will give me the address."

"Nobody in particular," said I, "so it does not matter; you can keep it and read it. It is a riddle; that is what has been amusing us so much. Lady Ursula has been making such absurd attempts to guess it. Good-bye, Lady Broadhem. Here is the servant come to say that my fly is at the door."

"Good gracious! Why, where are you going?" said she, evidently imagining that her daughter and I had had some thrilling episode, and that I was going away in a huff, so I determined to mystify her still more.

"Oh, only to Flityville to get everything ready; you know what a state the place is in. Now," and I looked tenderly into the amazed face of Lady Ursula, "I shall indeed have an object in putting it in order, and I shall expect you and Lady Ursula to come some day soon and suggest the improvements. I have only one request to make before leaving, and I do so, Lady Ursula, in the presence of your mother and sister; and that is, that until I see you again, the subject of our conversation just now may never be alluded to between yourselves. Trust in me, Lady Broadhem," I said, taking her hand affectionately, "and promise me you will not ask Lady Ursula what I have just told her; if you do," I whispered, "you will spoil all," and I looked happy and mysterious. "Do you promise?"

"I do," said Lady Broadhem.

"And now, Lady Ursula," I said, crossing over to her and taking her hand, "once more good-bye, and"—I went on in so low a tone that it was impossible for Lady Broadhem to overhear it, but it made her feel sure that all was arranged between us—"you have got the most terrible secret of my life. I know I can trust you. You have seen me"—and I formed the word with my lips rather than uttered it with my breath—"MAD! Hush!" for Lady Ursula gave a quick exclamation, and almost fainted with alarm; "I am myself again now. Remember my happiness is in your keeping"—this out loud for Lady Broadhem's benefit. "I am going to say good-bye to Lady Dickiefield, and you shall hear from me when I can receive you at Flityville."

I am endowed with a somewhat remarkable faculty, which I have not been in the habit of alluding to, partly because my friends think me ridiculous if I do, and partly because I never could see any use in it, but I do nevertheless possess the power of seeing in the dark. Not after the manner of cats—the objects which actually exist—but images which sometimes appear as the condensations of a white misty-looking substance, and sometimes take a distinctly bright luminous appearance. As I gaze into absolute darkness, I first see a cloud, which gradually seems to solidify into a shape, either of an animal or some definite object. In the case of the more brilliant image, the appearance is immediate and evanescent. It comes and goes like a flash, and the subject is generally significant and beautiful. Perhaps some of my readers may be familiar with this phenomenon, and may account for it as being the result of what they call imagination, which is only putting the difficulty one step back; or may adopt the wiser course which I have followed, and not endeavour to account for it at all. Whatever be its origin, the fact remains, and I only advert to it now, as it is the best illustration I can think of to describe the mental process through which I passed in the train on my way to Flityville. My mind seemed at first a white mist—a blank sheet of paper. My interview with Lady Ursula had produced this effect upon it. Gradually, and quite unconsciously to myself, so far as any mental effort was concerned, my thoughts seemed to condense into a definite plan of action; now and then a brilliant idea would appear like a flash, and vanish sometimes before I could catch it; but in so far as the complication in which Grandon, Ursula, the Broadhem family, and myself were concerned, I seemed to see my way, or at all events to feel sure that my way would be shown to me, if I let my inspirations guide me. When once one achieves this thorough confidence in one's inspirations, the journey of life becomes simplified. You never wonder what is round the next corner, and begin to prepare for unknown contingencies; but you wait till the corner is turned, and the contingency arrives, and passively allow your mind to crystallise itself into a plan of action. At this moment, of course, I have no more notion what is going to happen to me than you have. Divest your mind, my friend, that I know anything more of the plot of this story of my life which you are reading than you do. I positively have not the slightest idea what either I or any of the ladies and gentlemen to whom I have introduced you are likely to do, or how it is all going to end. I have told you the mental process under which I act; and, of course, this is the mere record of those inspirations. Very often the most unlikely things occur to me all of a sudden: thus, while my mind was, as it were, trifling with the events which I have recounted, and throwing them into a variety of combinations, it flashed upon me in the most irrelevant manner that I would send £4000 anonymously to the Bishop of London's fund. In another second the unconscious train of thought which led me to this determination revealed itself. "Here," said I, "have I been attacking this poor colonial bishop and the Establishment to which he belongs, and what have I given him in return? I expose the abuses of his theological and ecclesiastical system, but I provide him with no remedy. I fling one big stone at the crystal palace in which Protestantism is shrivelling away, and another big stone at the crystal palace in which Catholicism is rotting, and I offer them in exchange the cucumber-frame under which I am myself squatting uncomfortably. I owe them an apology. Unfortunately I have not yet found either the man or the body of men who do not prefer hard cash to an apology—provided, of course, it be properly proportioned to the susceptibility of their feelings or the delicacy of their sense of honour. Fairly, now," I asked myself, "if it was put to the Bench of Bishops, would they consider £5000 sufficient to compensate the Church for the expressions I made use of to one of their order?"

"More than sufficient," myself replied. "Then we will make it four thousand." But the whole merit of the action lies in the anonymous, and so nobody knows till they read this who it was made that munificent donation. That I should have afterwards changed my mind, and answered the advertisement of the committee, which appeared in the "agony" column of the 'Times,' who wanted to know how I wished the money applied, by a request that it should be paid back to my account at the Bank, does not affect the question; I merely wished to show the nature of my impulses, and the readiness with which I act upon them.

Some days elapsed after my arrival at Flityville before I felt moved to write to Grandon. The fact is, I was writing this record of my trials for the world in general, and did not know what to say to him in particular. At length, feeling that I owed him an explanation, I wrote as follows:—

"FLITYVILLE, *March 19*.

"You are doubtless surprised, my dear fellow," I began, "at my turning myself into a hermit at this most inopportune season of the year; but the fact is, that shortly after you left Dickiefield, I became so deeply impressed with the responsibility of the great work I had undertaken, that I perceived that a period of retirement and repose was absolutely necessary with a view to the elaboration of some system which should enable me to grapple with the great moral and social questions upon which I am engaged.

"Diverting my anxious gaze from Christendom generally, I concentrated it upon my own country, in the hope that I might discover the root of its disease. Morbid activity of the national brain, utterly deranged action of the national heart. Those were the symptoms—unmistakable. Proximate cause also not difficult to arrive at. Due to the noxious influence of tall chimneys upon broad acres, whereby the commercial effluvium of the Plutocracy has impregnated the upper atmosphere, and overpowered the enfeebled and enervated faculties of the aristocracy; lust of gain has supervened upon love of ease. Hence the utter absence of those noble and generous impulses which are the true indications of healthy national life. Expediency has taken the place of principle; conscience has been crushed out of the system by calculation. The life-blood of the country, instead of bounding along its veins, creeps sluggishly through them, till it threatens to stagnate altogether, and congestion becomes imminent.

"Looked at from what I may term 'externals,' we simply present to the world at large the ignoble spectacle of a nation of usurers trembling over our money-bags; looked at from internals, I perceive that we are suffering from a moral opiate, to the action of which I attribute the unhappy complaints that I have endeavoured to describe. This pernicious narcotic has been absorbed by us for hundreds of years unsuspected and unperceived under the guise of a popular theology. We have become so steeped in the insane delusion, now many centuries old, that we are a Christian nation, that I anticipate with dread the reaction which will take place when men awaken to the true character of the religious quackery with which they have been duped, and, overlooking in their frenzy the distinction which exists between ancient and modern Christianity, will repudiate the former with horror, which, after all, does not deserve to be condemned, for it has never yet been tried as a political system in any country. Individuals only profess to be theoretically governed by it. Nor would it be possible, as society is at present constituted, for any man to carry out its principles in daily life. That any statesman would be instantly ruined who should openly announce that he intended to govern the country on purely Christian principles, may be made clear to the simplest comprehension. For instance, imagine our Foreign Minister getting up in the House of Commons and justifying his last stroke of foreign policy upon the ground that we should 'love our neighbours better than ourselves, or penning a despatch to any power that we felt 'persecuted' by blessing it. When do we even do good to anybody in our national capacity, much less to them 'that hate us'? We certainly pray like Chinamen when we want to propitiate an angry Deity about the cattle-plague; but who ever heard of 'a form of prayer to be used' for nations 'who despitefully use us.' Fancy the Chancellor of the Exchequer informing us that instead of laying up for the nation treasures upon earth, he proposed realising all that the country possessed and giving it to the poor. Christian Churchmen and statesmen do not therefore sufficiently believe in the power and efficacy of the Christian moral code to trust the nation to it alone. Hence they have invented ecclesiastical organisations and theological dogmas as anodynes; and the people have been lulled into security by the singular notion, that if they supported the one and professed to believe in the other, they were different from either Mohammedans or Bhuddists. In a word, it is the curse of England that its intellect can see truths which its heart will not embody. The more I think of it the more I am disposed to risk the assertion, that if, as is supposed, the moral code called Christian is divine, it is only not practicable, literally, by the nation for lack of national heart-faith. I tell you this in confidence, for I am already considered so wild and visionary upon all these matters, and so thoroughly unsound, that I should not like it to be generally known, for fear of its injuring my political prospects. In the mean time it will very much assist me in arriving at some of my conclusions, if you will kindly procure for me, from any leading member of the Legislature, lay or clerical, answers to the following questions:—

"First, Whether Jonah could possibly have had anything to say to Nineveh which would not apply with equal force to this Christian metropolis?—and if so, What?

"Second, Specify the sins which were probably committed in Chorazin or Bethsaida, but which have not yet been perpetrated in London.

"Third, As statecraft (assisted by priestcraft) consists not in making the State better but richer, explain why it is easier for a collection of rich men—called a nation—to be saved, than for a camel to go through the eye of a needle, but not so easy for one man.

"Fourth, Does the saying that the love of money is the root of all evil apply to a nation as well as to an individual?—and if not, how does it happen that the more we accumulate wealth, the more we increase poverty and misery and crime?

"That is enough for the present. But oh! what a string of questions I could propound to these stumbling pagans, stupefied by the fatuous superstition that their country is safer than other countries which have come to judgment, because they are called by a particular name! Is there among them all not the faintest consciousness of an impending doom? or is the potency of the drug such that it is impossible to raise a cry loud enough to rouse them? Why will they go on vainly trying to solve the impossible problem of Government, never seeing that whatever system is introduced is merely a rearrangement of sinners; that voters are like cards—the more you shuffle them the dirtier they get; and that it is of no use agitating for a reform in the franchise without first agitating for a reform in the consciences of those who are to exercise it, and in the fundamental principles of the policy upon which we are to be governed.

"Wisely saith the greatest poet of the age, as yet, alas! unknown to fame:—

"Reformers fail because they change the letter,And not the spirit, of the world's design.Tyrant and slave create the scourge and fetter—As is the worshipper, will be the shrine.The ideal fails, though perfect were the plan,World-harmony springs through the perfect man.

We burn out life in hot impatient striving;We dash ourselves against the hostile spears:The bale-tree, that our naked hands are riving,Unites to crush us. Ere our manhood's years,We sow the rifled blossoms of the prime,Then fruitlessly are gathered out of time.

We seek to change souls all unripe for changes;We build upon a treacherous human soilOf moral quicksand, and the world avengesIts crime upon us, while we vainly toil.In the black coal-pit of the popular heartRain falls, light kindles, but no flowers upstart.

Know this! For men of ignoble affection,The social scheme that is, were better farThan the orbed sun's most exquisite perfection,Man needs not heaven till he revolves a star.Why seek to win the mad world from its strife?Grow perfect in the sanity of life."[2]

"Ah, my dear friend! how often, from my humble seat below the gangway, have I gazed upon the Treasury Bench, and wondered how it was that right hon. gentlemen, struggling to retain their dignity by sitting on each other's knees, did not perceive that the reason why great reforms perpetually fail is, not because they have not their root in some radical injustice—not because the despotisms against which they rise are in themselves right—but because those who attempt to inaugurate new and better conditions upon the surfaces of society are themselves, for the most part, desolate, darkened, and chaotic within! I am under the impression, therefore, that no reform-agitation will ever do good which is not preceded by an agitation, throughout the length and breadth of the land, in favour of the introduction, for the first time, of this old original moral code, not merely into the government of the country, but into the life of every individual. Unless that is done, and done speedily, those who are now morally stupefied will die in their torpor, and the rest who are harmless lunatics will become gibbering and shrieking demoniacs.—

Yours affectionately,

"F. V."

I had become so absorbed by the train of considerations into which I had been led, that I never thought of mentioning to Grandon the circumstances which attended my departure from Dickiefield. It was not until after I had posted my letter that it occurred to me how singular, considering the last words which passed between us, this silence would appear. If to be odd has its drawbacks, it also has its advantages; and I felt that Grandon would be as unable to draw any conclusions from my silence as from any other erratic act of my life. After all, what could I have said? It will be time, I thought, to venture upon that very delicate ground when I get his reply. But this I was destined never to receive, and the questions I had propounded are likely to remain unanswered, for on the very next day I received the following telegram from Lady Broadhem:—

"Your immediate presence here is absolutely necessary. Delay will be fatal.

"Mary Broadhem.

"Grosvenor Square, *20th March.*"

PART III.

SUICIDE.

Piccadilly, *April.*

Considering the extent to which I have been digressing, it will be perhaps desirable, before I plunge again into the stormy current of my narrative, to define in a few words what, in the language of diplomacy, is termed "the situation." After I have done so, I shall feel much obliged if you will kindly "grasp" it. Briefly, it is as follows: I am telegraphed for in frantic terms by an old lady who is under the firm impression that I am engaged to be married to her daughter. I am violently in love with that daughter, but for certain reasons I have felt it my duty to account for my extraordinary conduct by informing her confidentially that I have occasional fits of temporary insanity. That daughter, I am positively assured by her mother, is no less violently attached to my most dear and intimate friend. My most dear and intimate friend returns the affection. Mamma threatens that if I do not marry her daughter, rather than allow my most dear and intimate friend to do so, she will ally the young lady to an affluent native of Bombay. So much is known. On the following points I am still in the dark:—

First, What on earth does Lady Broadhem mean by telling me to come immediately, as delay may be fatal?—to whom? to me or to Lady Ursula, or herself? My knowledge of her ladyship induces me to incline towards the latter hypothesis; the suspense is, however, none the less trying.

Second, Does Lady Ursula imagine that I know how she and Grandon feel towards each other?

Third, Is Grandon under the impression that I have actually proposed and been accepted by Lady Ursula?

Fourth, Does my conduct occasionally amount to something more than eccentricity or not?

Fifth—and this was very unpleasant—Shall I find Grandon at our joint abode? And if so, what shall I say to him?

Sixth, Have Grandon and Lady Ursula met, and did anything pass between them?

Thank goodness Grandon was at the House. So, after a hurried toilet, I went on to Grosvenor Square. The young ladies were both out. Lady Bridget had taken advantage of the *chaperonage* of a newly-married rather fast female cousin, to go to a ball. Lady Ursula had gone to a solitary tea with a crabbed old aunt. Lady Broadhem was in her own sitting-room, lying on a couch behind a table covered with papers. She looked wearily up when I entered, and held out a thin hand for me to do what I liked with. "How good of you to come, dear Frank!" she said. It was the first time she had ever called me Frank, and I knew she expected me to acknowledge it by pressing her fingers, so I squeezed them affectionately. "Broadhem said if I wanted to make sure of you I ought to have brought Ursula's name into the telegraph, but I told him her mother's would do as well."

"What does the——" I am afraid I mentally said 'old girl'—"want, I wonder? It must be really serious, or she would have shammed agitation. There is something about this oily calm which is rather portentous. Then she has taken care to have every member of the family out of the house. What is she ringing the bell for now?"

"Tell Lady Ursula when she comes home that I am engaged particularly, and will come up and see her in her bedroom before she goes to bed," said Lady Broadhem to the servant who answered it.

"Does not Lady Ursula know of my having come to town in answer to your summons?" I asked.

"No, dear child; why should I inflict my troubles upon her? Even Broadhem, to whom I was obliged to speak more openly, only suspects the real state of the case. I have reserved my full confidence for my future son-in-law."

I lifted up my eyes with a rapturous expression, and played with a paper-knife. She wanted me to help her on with an obvious remark, which I declined to make; so, after a pause, she went on, with a deep sigh,——

"What sad news we keep on getting of those poor dear Confederates, Frank!"

"Let us hope they will recover," said I, encouragingly.

"Oh, but they do keep on falling so, it is quite dreadful."

"There was no great number of them fell at Wilmington."

"How stupid I am!" she said; "my poor mind gets quite bewildered. I was thinking of stock, not men; they went down again three more yesterday, and my broker declines altogether to carry them on from one account to another any more. I bought at 60, and they have done nothing but go down ever since. I generally go by Lord Staggerton's advice, and he recommended me to sell a bear some months ago; but that stupid little Spiffy Goldtip insisted that it was only a temporary depression, and now he says how could he know that President Davis would replace Johnston by Hood."

"Very tiresome of Davis: but you should have employed more than one broker," I remarked. "Persons of limited capital and speculative tendencies should operate mysteriously. Your right hand should not know what your left hand is doing."

"Hush, Frank! you can surely be business-like without being profane. I was completely in Spiffy's hands; Lady Mundane told me she always let him do for her, and"—here Lady Broadhem lowered her voice—"I *know* he has access to the best sources of information. I used to employ Staggerton, but he is so selfish that he never told me the best things; besides which, of course, I was obliged to have him constantly to dinner; and his great delight was always to say things which were calculated to shock my religious friends. Moreover, he has lately been doing more as a promoter of new companies than in buying and selling. Now Spiffy is so very useful in society, and has so much tact, that although there are all kinds of stories against him, still I did not think there was any sufficient reason to shut him out of the house. There was quite a set made against the poor little man at one time—worldly people are so hard and uncharitable; so, partly for the sake of his aunt, Lady Spiffington, who was my dear friend, and partly, indeed, because Staggerton had really become useless and intolerable, I put my affairs entirely into Spiffy's hands."

"And the result is?" I asked.

"That I must pay up £27,000 to-morrow," said Lady Broadhem, with the impenitent sigh of a hardened criminal.

"You should have kept his lordship to act as a check on the Honourable Spiffington," I said; "but I cannot advise now, unless I know everything."

A faint tinge suffused Lady Broadhem's cheek as she said, "What more do you want to know?"

"Exactly what money you possess, and exactly how it is invested."

"I don't see that that is at all necessary. Here is Spiffington's letter, from which you will see how much I must pay to-morrow; my assurance that I cannot produce so large a sum at such short notice is enough."

"You can surely have no difficulty in finding some one who would lend you the money, provided you were to pay a sufficiently high rate of interest."

The tinge which had not left Lady Broadhem's cheek deepened as she answered me, "Frank, it was on no hasty impulse that I telegraphed for you. I do not feel bound to enter into all the details of my private affairs, but I do feel that if there is one man in the world upon whom, at such a crisis, I have a right to rely, it is he to whom I have promised my daughter, and who professes to be devotedly attached to her."

"In short, Lady Broadhem," said I, rising and taking up my hat, "you are willing to part with your daughter to me on condition of my paying a first instalment of £27,000 down, with the prospect of 'calls' to an unlimited extent looming in the background. I doubt whether you will find Chundango prepared to go into such a very hazardous speculation, but I should recommend you to apply to him."

At that moment I heard Lady Ursula's voice in the hall, and the rustle of her dress as she went up-stairs. I was on my way to the door, but I stopped abruptly, and turned upon Lady Broadhem. She was saying something to which I was not attending, but now was suddenly paralysed and silenced as I looked at her fixedly. If a glance can convey meaning, I flatter myself my eyes were not devoid of expression at that moment. "What!" I thought, "is it reserved for the mother of the girl I love to make me call her 'a hazardous speculation'?" It is impossible for me to describe the intensity of the hatred which I felt at this moment for the woman who had caused me for one second to think of Ursula as a marketable commodity, who should be offered for purchase to an Oriental adventurer. The only being I despised more than Lady Broadhem was myself;— because she chose to take my angel off the pedestal on which I had placed her and throw her into the dirt, was I calmly to acquiesce in the proceeding? The storm raging within me seemed gradually to blind me to external objects; my great love was battling with remorse, indignation, and despair; and I stood wavering and distracted, looking, as it were, within for rest and without for comfort, till the light seemed to leave my eyes, and the fire which had flashed from them for a moment became suddenly extinguished.

I was recalled to consciousness by an exclamation from Lady Broadhem. "Heavens, Frank, don't stare so wildly—you quite frighten me! I have only asked for your advice, and you make use of expressions and fly off in a manner which nothing but the excitability of your temperament can excuse. I assure you I am worried enough without having my cares added to by your unkindness. There, if you want to know the exact state of my affairs, look through my papers—you will find I am a woman of business; and I have got an accurate list which I shall be able to explain. Of course all the more important original documents are at my solicitor's."

I sat moodily down without answering this semi-conciliatory, semi-plaintive speech. I did not even take the trouble to analyse it. I felt morally and physically exhausted. The long journey, the suspense, and this *dénouement*, had prostrated me. I took up the papers Lady Broadhem offered me, and turned them vacantly over. I read the list, but failed to attach any meaning to the items over which my gaze listlessly wandered. I felt that Lady Broadhem was watching me curiously, but every effort I made to grasp the details before me failed hopelessly. At last I threw the packet down in despair, and, leaning over the table, clasped my bursting forehead with my hands.

"Dear Frank," said Lady Broadhem, and for the first time her voice betrayed signs of genuine emotion, "I know I have been very imprudent, but I did it all for the best. You can understand now why I hesitated to tell you everything at first. You don't know how much it has cost me, and to what means I am obliged to resort to keep up my courage; besides, I have got into such a habit of concealment that I could not bear that even you should know the desperate state of our affairs, though I had no idea that in so short a time you could have unravelled such complicated accounts and arrived at the terrible result. Perhaps you would like me to leave you for a few moments. I will go and say good-night to Ursula, whom I heard going up-stairs just now."

I heard Lady Broadhem leave the room, but did not raise my head, and indeed only slowly comprehended the purport of her last speech. As it dawned upon me, the hopelessness of the whole situation seemed to overwhelm me. Chaos and ruin like gaunt spectres stared me in the face! What mattered it if the Broadhem family were bankrupt in estate, if I was to become bankrupt in mind? What matter if they lost all their worldly possessions? Had I not lost all hope of Ursula since I had heard of her attachment to Grandon, and with her every generous impulse of my nature? Why should I save the family, even if I could? Why in this desert of my existence spend a fortune on an oasis I was forbidden ever to enter or enjoy? Why should I bring offerings to the shrine at which I might never worship? The whole temple that enclosed it was tottering. Instead of helping to prop it up, why not, like Samson, drag it down and let it bury me in its ruin? I threw myself on the couch from which Lady Broadhem had risen, and, turning my face to the wall, longed with an intense desire for an eternal release. At that moment my hand, which I had thrust under the pillow, came in contact with something hard and cold. I drew it out, and was startled to find that it was a small vial labelled "POISON." I am not naturally superstitious, but this immediate response to my thoughts seemed an indication so direct as to be almost supernatural. I had hardly framed in definite terms the idea of a suicide which should at once end my agony, when the means thereto were actually placed in my very hand. Even had I doubted, the inward sense, the inspiration to which I trust, and which has never yet failed me, said, Drink! It even whispered aloud, Drink! From every corner of the room came soft pleasant murmurs of the same word. Beautiful sirens floating round me bade me drink. Every thought of moral evil vanished in connection with this final act. I looked forward with rapture to the long sleep before me, and with a smile of the most intense and fervent gratitude I raised the bottle to my lips. I remember thinking at the moment, "The smile is very important—it shall play upon my lips to the end. Ursula, I die happy, for my last thought is, that in the spirit I shall soon revisit thee," and the liquid trickled slowly down my throat. It was not until I had drained the last drop that I suddenly recognised the taste. It was the "pick-me-up" I always get at Harris's, the apothecary in St James's Street, when my fit of nervous exhaustion come on, but there seemed rather more of the spirituous ingredient in it than usual. The life-stream began to tingle back through all my fibres—my miseries took grotesque forms. "Ha! ha! Lady Broadhem! the means you take to keep up your courage, which you so delicately alluded to just now, have come in most opportunely. What a fool I was to make mountains out of molehills, and call the little ills of life miseries! We will soon see what these little imprudences are the old lady talks of." And I took up the papers with a hand rapidly becoming steady, and glanced over them with an eye no longer confused and dim. Oh the pleasure of the sensation of this gradual recovery of vigour of mind and force of body!

I was engaged in this task, and making the most singular and startling discoveries, the nature of which I shall shortly disclose, when I heard Lady Broadhem coming down-stairs. I felt so angry with her for having been the means of tempting me to commit a great sin, and for the trouble she was causing me generally, that I followed the first impulse which my imagination suggested as the best means of revenging myself upon her. Accordingly, when the door opened, she found me stretched at full length on the sofa, my form rigid, my face fixed, my eyes staring, my hands clenched, and my whole attitude as nearly that of a person in a fit as I had time to make it.

"Gracious, what is the matter?" said she.

My lips seemed with difficulty to form the word "poison."

"Frank, speak to me!" and she seized my hand, which was not so cold as I could have wished it, but which fell helplessly by my side as she let it drop.

"Poison!" I this time muttered audibly.

"Where did you get it?" said she, snappishly. For it began to dawn upon her that I was not poisoned at all, but had discovered her secret. I turned my thumb languidly in the direction of under the pillow. She hastily thrust in her hand and pulled out the empty bottle. "You fool"—she actually used this expression; I have heard other ladies do the same—"you fool," and she was literally furious, "what did you go poking under the pillow for? You are no more poisoned than I am; it is a draught I am obliged to take for nervous depression, and your imagination has almost frightened you into a fit. I put 'poison' on it to keep the servants from prying. Come, get up, be a man—do," and Lady Broadhem gave me her hand, in consideration for my weakness to help myself up by.

"Dearest Lady Broadhem," said I, pressing it to my lips, "I cannot tell what comfort you give me. I was just beginning to regret the world I thought I was about to leave for ever, when your assurance that I have not taken poison, but a tonic, makes me feel as grateful to you as if you had saved my life. I confess that, when I found that you considered your affairs to be so desperate that you had provided the most effectual mode of escape from them, I envied the superior foresight which you had displayed, and determined to repair my error. If it is worth dear Lady Broadhem's while to poison herself, I thought, it is surely worth mine. But, after all, suicide is a cowardly act either in a man or a woman; better far face the ills of life with the aid of stimulants, than fly for refuge in the agony of a financial crisis to the shop of an apothecary."

"You are an incomprehensible creature, Frank," said Lady Broadhem; "I am sure I hope for her own sake that Ursula will understand you better than I do; but as your humours are uncertain, and you seem able to go into these affairs now, I think we had better not waste any more time; only I do wish" (with a wistful glance at the bottle) "you would provide yourself with your own draughts in future."

"How lucky," thought I, as I put on a business-like air, and methodically began arranging the papers according to their docquets. "Now, if it had been just the other way, and her ladyship had taken the draught instead of me, how completely I should have been at her mercy? Now I am master of the situation."

"'Greek loan, thirty thousand,'" I read, going down the list; "I am afraid this is rather a losing business. I see they have been already held over for some months. I suppose some of the £27,000 is to be absorbed there."

"Yes," said Lady Broadhem; "because if I can carry on for another fortnight, I have got information which makes it certain I shall recover on them."

"What is this? five hundred pounds' worth of dollar bonds?" I went on.

"Oh, I only lost a few pounds on them. I bought them at threepence apiece and sold them at twopence. Spiffy got me to take them off his hands, and, in fact, made a great favour of it, as he says there is nothing people make money more surely out of than dollar bonds."

"Bubbs's Eating-house and Cigar Divan Company, Holborn. Well, there is a strong direction. How do you come by so many shares?"

"Lord Staggerton was one of the promoters, and had them allotted to me," said Lady Broadhem. "He also was kind enough to put me into two Turkish baths, a monster hotel, and a music-hall. You will see that I lost heavily in the Turkish baths and the hotel, but the music-hall is paying well. Spiffy says I ought never to stay so long in anything as I do; in and out again, if it is only half a per cent, is his system; but Staggerton used to look after my interests, and managed them very successfully. I am afraid that all my troubles commenced when I quarrelled with him. He is now promoting two companies which I hear most highly spoken of, but he says I must take my chance with others about shares, and he won't advise me in the matter. One is 'The Metropolitan Crossing-Sweeping Company,' of which he's to be chairman, and the other is the 'Seaside Bathing-Machine Company.' Spiffy says they will both fail, because Staggerton has not the means of having them properly brought out. Bodwinkle won't speak to him, and unless either he or the Credit Foncier bring a thing out, there is not the least chance of its taking with the public. They don't so much look at the merits of the speculation as at the way in which it is put before them; and with this system of rigging the market, so many people go in like me only to get out again, that it is becoming more and more difficult every day to start anything new. Oh dear," said Lady Broadhem, "how exhausted it always makes me to talk 'City!' I only want to show you that I understand what I am about, and that if you can only help to tide me over this crisis, something will surely turn up a prize."

"I know you disapprove of cards, but perhaps you will allow me to suggest the word 'trump' as being more expressive than 'prize,'" I said. "Well, now we have got through the companies, what have we here? Why, Lady Broadhem, you have positively taken no less than seven unfurnished houses this year. What on earth do you intend to do with them all?"

"My dear Frank, where have you been living for the last few years? Do with them? Exactly what dozens of smart people, with very little to live on, do with houses—let them, to be sure. I made £1100 last year in four houses, and all by adding it on to the premiums. I don't like furnishing and putting it in the rent. In the first place, one is apt to have disagreeable squabbles about the furniture, which, however good you give people, they always say is shabby; and in the second, you get much more into the hands of the house-agents."

"Well, but," I said, "here is one of the largest houses in London—rent, unfurnished, £1500 a-year. That is rather hazardous: who do you expect will take that?"

"Oh, that is the safest speculation of them all," said Lady Broadhem. "I had an infinity of trouble to get it. Spiffy first suggested the plan to me, and we found it succeed admirably last year. It was we who brought out Mrs Gorgon Tompkins and her daughters. She took the house from me at my own rent on condition that Spiffy managed her balls, and got all the best people in London to go to them. This year we are going to bring out the Bodwinkles. It will be much easier, because she is young, and has no family. He, you know, is a man of immense wealth in the City—in fact, as I said before, his name is almost essential to the success of any new company. I told his wife I could have nothing to do with them unless he came into Parliament, for they are horridly vulgar, and they were bound to do what they could for themselves before I could think of taking them up. Lady Mundane positively refused to have anything to do with them, and, in fact, I live so little in the world, though I keep it up to some extent for the sake of my girls, that it was quite an accident my hearing of them. Now, however, he has got into the House of Commons, and it is arranged that she is to take the house, and Bodwinkle is to help Spiffy in City matters, on condition that he gets all Lady Mundane's list to her first party. Poor Spiffy is a little nervous, as Bodwinkle actually wanted to put it in writing on a stamped paper; but he is so immensely useful to society, that the least people can do is to be good-natured on an occasion of this kind."

"No fear of them," said I; "if Bodwinkle is the only man who can launch a company in the City, no one can compete with Spiffy in launching a snob in Mayfair. But I thought you never went to balls."

"I never do; but because I do not approve of dancing, there is no reason why I should not let houses for the purpose. You might as well say a religious banker ought not to open an account with a theatre, or a good brewer live by his beer, because some people drink too much of it. If any one was to leave a gin-palace to me in a legacy, I should not refuse the rent."

"Any more than you do the interest of your shares in the music-hall. And now," said I, coolly, gathering up all her papers and putting them in my pocket, "as it is past one o'clock, and I see you are tired, I will take these away with me, and let you know to-morrow what I think had better be done under the circumstances."

"What are you doing, Frank? what an unheard-of proceeding! I insist upon your leaving my papers here."

"If I do, you must look elsewhere for the money. No, Lady Broadhem"—I felt that my moral ascendancy was increasing every moment, and that I should never have such another opportunity of establishing it—"we had better understand each other clearly. You regard me at this moment in the light of your future son-in-law, and in that capacity expect me to extricate you and your family from your financial difficulties. Now I am quite capable of 'behaving badly,' as the world calls it, at the shortest notice. I told you at Dickiefield that I was totally without principle, and we are both trusting to Ursula to reform me. But I will relinquish the pleasure of paying your debts, and the advantage of being reformed by your daughter, unless you agree to my terms."

"And they are?" said her ladyship, doggedly.

"First, that from this evening you put the entire management of your affairs into my hands, and, as a preliminary measure, allow me to take away these papers, giving me a note to your lawyer authorising him to follow my instructions in everything; and, secondly, that you never, under any pretence, enter into any company or speculation of any kind except with my permission."

A glance of very evil meaning shot across her ladyship's eyes as they met mine after this speech, but I frightened it away by the savageness of my gaze, till she was literally obliged to put her hand up to her forehead. The crisis was exciting me, for Ursula was at stake, and it was just possible my conditions might be refused; but I felt the magnetism of my will concentrating itself in my eyes as if they were burning-glasses. It seemed to dash itself upon the reefs and barriers of Lady Broadhem's rocky nature; the inner forces of our organisms were engaged in a decisive struggle for the mastery; but the field of battle was in her, not in me. I had invaded the enemy's country, and her frontier was as long and difficult to defend as ours is in Canada. So I kept on pouring in mesmeric reinforcements, as she sat with her head bent, and her whole moral being in turmoil. Never before had any man ventured to dictate to this veteran campaigner. The late Lord had been accustomed to regard her as infallible, and Broadhem has not yet known the pleasures of independence. She never had friends who were not servile, or permitted herself to be contradicted, except by a few privileged ecclesiastics, and then only in unctuous and deprecatory tones. That I, of whom the world was accustomed to speak in terms of compassion, and whom she inwardly despised at this moment, should stand over her more unyielding and imperious than herself, caused her to experience a sensation nearly allied to suffocation. I seemed instinctively to follow the mental processes through which she was passing, and a certain consciousness that I did so demoralised her. Now, I felt, she is going to take me to task in a "sweet Christian spirit" about the state of my soul, and I brought up "will" reinforcements which I poured down upon her brain through the parting of her front, till she backed suddenly out of the position, and took up a hostile, I might almost say an abusive, attitude. Here again I met her with such a shower of invective, "uttered not, yet comprehended," that after a silent contest she gave this up too, and finally fell back on the flat rejection of me and my money altogether. This, I confess, was the critical moment. She took her hand down when she came to this mental resolution, and she looked at me, I thought, but it might have been imagination, demoniacally. What had I to oppose to it? My love for Ursula? No; that would soften me. My aversion to Lady Broadhem? No; for it was not so great as hers for me. For a moment I wavered; my will seemed paralysed; her gaze was becoming fascinating, while mine was getting clouded, till a mist seemed to conceal her from me altogether. And now, at the risk of being misunderstood and ridiculed, I feel bound to describe exactly the most remarkable occurrence of my life. At that moment I saw distinctly, in the luminous haze which surrounded me, a fiery cross. I have already said that objects of this kind often appeared to me in the dark, apropos of nothing; but upon no former occasion had a lighted room become dim, and a vision manifested itself within which seemed to answer to the involuntary invocation for assistance that I made when I found the powers of my own will beginning utterly to fail me; and, what was still more strange, never before had any such manifestation effected an immediate revolution in my sentiments. Up to that moment I had been internally fierce and overbearing in my resolution to subdue the nature with which I was contending, and I was actually defeated when I received this supernatural indication of assistance. Before the dazzling vision had vanished, it had conveyed its lesson of self-sacrifice, and created within me a new impulse, under the influence of which I solemnly vowed that if I triumphed now I should use my victory for the good not only of those I loved, but of her then sitting before me. The demon of my own nature, which had evidently been struggling with the demon of hers, suddenly deserted me, and his place seemed occupied by an angel of light, furnishing me with the powers of exorcism, which were to be gained only at the sacrifice of self. My very breath seemed instantly charged with prayers for her, at the moment I felt she regarded me with loathing and hate.

An ineffable calm pervaded my whole being. A sense of happiness and gratitude deprived the consciousness of the conquest which I had gained of any sentiment of exultation; on the contrary, I felt gentle and subdued myself—anxious to soothe and comfort her with that consolation I had just experienced. Ah, Lady Broadhem! at that moment, had I not been in the presence of a "saint," I should have fallen upon my knees. Perhaps as it was I might have done so, had she not suddenly leant back exhausted.

"Frank," she said, "I seem to have been dreaming. I am subject to fits of violent nervous depression, and the agitation of this scene has completely overcome me; my brain seems stunned, and all my faculties have become torpid. I can think of nothing more now, do what you like; all I want is to go to sleep. If you ring the bell in that corner, Jenkins will come down. Good-night; I shall see you to-morrow. Take the papers with you."

I took Lady Broadhem's hand—it was cold and clammy—and held it till her maid came down. She had already fallen into a half-mesmeric sleep, but was not conscious of her condition. I saw her safely on her way to her bedroom on the arm of her maid, and left the house with my pockets full of papers, more fresh and invigorated than I had felt for weeks. A new light had indeed dawned upon me. For the first time one of these "hallucinations," as medical men usually term them, to which I am subject, had contained a lesson. Not only had I profited from it upon the spot, but it had suggested to me an entirely new line of conduct in the great question which most nearly affected my own happiness, and seemed to guarantee me the strength of will and moral courage which should enable me to carry it out.

As I walked home, with the piercing March wind cutting me through, solemn thoughts and earnest aspirations arose within me, and, struggling into existence amid the wreck that seemed to strew the disturbed chambers of my brain, came the prayer of an old saint, which, in years gone by, had fixed itself permanently in some vacant niche of my mind:—

"Great God! I ask Thee for no meaner pelf,Than that I may not disappoint myself,That in my actions I may soar as highAs I can now discern with this clear eye;And next in value what Thy kindness lends,That I may greatly disappoint my friends,Howe'er they think or hope that it might be,They may not dream how Thou'st distinguished me;That my weak hand may equal my firm faith,And my life practise more than my tongue saith;That my low conduct may not show,Nor my relenting lines,That I Thy purpose did not know,Or overrated Thy designs."

Time alone will show whether the project I formed under the new influences which were now controlling me, will ever be realised.

There is one point which I have in common with Archimedes,—my most brilliant inspirations very often come to me in my tub, or while I am dressing. On the morning following the scene above described, I trusted to this moment to furnish me with an idea which should enable me to put my plan into operation, but I sought in vain.

In the first place, though I assumed in the presence of Lady Broadhem a thorough knowledge of the peculiar description of the transaction in which she was engaged, I feel bound not to conceal from my readers that I have made it a rule through life to confine my knowledge of business strictly to theory, and though I am as thoroughly conversant with the terms of the Stock Exchange as with the language of the swell mob, I avoid, in ordinary life, making use either of one or the other. Hence I have always treated debentures, stock, scrip, coupons, and all the jargon connected with such money-making and money-losing contrivances, as pertaining to the abstract science of finance; nor do I ever desire to know anything of them practically, feeling assured that the information thus acquired is of a character calculated to exercise an injurious influence upon the moral nature. I do not for a moment wish to reflect upon those honest individuals who devote their whole lives to the acquisition of money and nothing else. Had one of my own ancestors not done so, I should not now be the millionaire I am, and able to write thus of the pursuit of wealth. But let no man tell me that the supreme indifference to it which I entertain, does not place me upon a higher platform than a gold-hunter can possibly aspire to. When, therefore, I looked forward to an interview with the Honourable Spiffington Goldtip, I felt that I incurred a very serious responsibility. Not being versed in the Capel Court standard of morality, or being in the habit of treading those delicate lines upon which Spiffy had learnt to balance himself so gracefully, I might, instead of doing him good, be the means of encouraging him in that pecuniary scramble which enabled him to gain a precarious livelihood.

"After all," I thought, "why not hover about the City with one's hands full of gold, as one used to after dinner at Greenwich, when showers of copper delighted the ragged crowd beneath, and have the fun of seeing all the mud-larking Spiffys, fashionable and snobbish, scrambling in wild confusion, and rolling fraternally over each other in the dirt? If I can't convert them, if I must be 'done' by them, I will 'do' to them as I would be 'done' by; and rather than leave them to perish, will adopt an extreme measure, and keep on suffocating them with the mud they delight to revel in, till they cry aloud for help. What a pleasure it would be to wash Spiffy all over afterwards, and start him fresh and sweet in a new line of life!" As I said before, I was in my tub myself as I made this appropriate reflection; then my thoughts involuntarily reverted to Chundango. When I had threatened Lady Broadhem with the mercenary spirit of that distinguished Oriental, I inwardly doubted whether, indeed, it were possible for her to propose any pecuniary sacrifice which he was not prepared to make, in order to gain the social prize upon which he had set his heart; and I dreaded lest I should have driven her in despair to have recourse to this "dark" alternative,—whether, in order to save the Broadhem family from ruin and disgrace—for I suspected that the papers I had carried away contained evidence that the one was as possible as the other—Ursula would accede to the pressure of the family generally, and of her mother in particular, whose wish none of her children had ever dared to thwart, was a consideration which caused me acute anxiety. I must prepare myself shortly for a conversation on the subject with Grandon. What should I say to him? Granting that the means occasionally justify the end, which I do not admit, what would be the use of making a false statement either in the sense that I was, or that I was not, going to marry Ursula? If I said I was, he would think me a traitor and her a jilt; if I said I was not, I must go on and tell him that the family would be ruined and disgraced, or that she must marry Chundango to save it. He would obtain comfort neither way. He had evidently not seen the Broadhems, and was therefore sure now to be in blissful ignorance that anything has happened at all. Better leave him so. If he is convinced that Ursula loves him, he would never dream of her accepting me. Even had our acquaintance been longer than it was, before I was so mad as to think of proposing to her, the best thing I can do is certainly to hold my tongue; but then, I thought, how will he account for my reserve? what can he think except that it arises from an unworthy motive?—and I brushed my hair viciously. At that instant I heard a thump at the door, and before I could answer, in walked the subject of my meditation.

"Well, my dear old fellow," said Grandon, as he grasped my hand warmly, "how mysterious and spasmodic you have been in your movements! I was afraid even now, if I had not invaded the sanctity of your dressing-room, that you would have slipped through my fingers. I know you have a great deal to tell me, of interest to us both, and we are too fast friends to hesitate to confide in each other on any matters which affect our happiness. True men never have any reticence as between themselves; they only have recourse to that armour when they happen to be cursed with false friends." I cannot describe my feelings during this speech. How on earth was I to avoid reticence? how show him that I loved and trusted him when I had just been elaborately devising a speech which should tell him nothing? and I thought of our school and then our college days—how I never seemed to be like other boys or other men of my own age—and how when nobody understood me Grandon did, and how when nobody defended my peculiarities Grandon did—how he protected and advised me at first out of sheer compassion, until at last I had become as a younger brother to him. How distressed he was when I gave up diplomacy, and how anxious during the five years that I was exploring in the Far West and gold-digging in Australia! and how nothing but his letters ever induced me to leave the wild reckless life that possessed such a wonderful charm for me; and how he bore with my wilfulness and vanity—for the faults of my character at such moments would become painfully apparent to me; and how now I was going to return it all, by allowing him to suppose that I had deliberately plotted against his happiness, and ruthlessly sapped the solid foundations upon which our life's friendship had been built. He saw these painful thoughts reflected but too accurately upon my face, for he had been accustomed to read it for so many years, and he smiled a look of encouragement and kindliness. "Come," he said, "I will tell you exactly, first, everything I suspect, and then everything I know, and then what I think about it, so that you will have as little of the labour of revelation as possible. First of all, I suspect that you imagine that I had proposed to Lady Ursula Newlyte before we met the other day at Dickiefield: I need not say that in that case I should have told you as much upon the evening we parted; I pledge you my word I have never uttered a syllable to Lady Ursula from which she could suspect the state of my feelings towards her, and she has never given me any indication that she returned my affection; I therefore did not mention myself when you told me your intention of proposing to her at Dickiefield; I only do so now in consequence of a letter which I received from Lady Broadhem last night."

"A letter from Lady Broadhem?" said I, aghast.

"Yes," he said, "in which she encloses a copy of one of yours containing a proposal to Lady Ursula, and informs me that you were aware, when you made it, of the difficulties you might have to encounter through me. She goes on to say that, whatever may have been her daughter's feelings towards me at one time, they have completely changed, as she at once accepted you; and she winds up with the rather unnecessary remark that this is the less to be regretted by me, as under no circumstances would I have obtained either her consent or that of Lord Broadhem. And so," my poor friend went on, but his lips were quivering, and I turned away my eyes to avoid seeing the effort it cost him—"and so, you see, my dear Frank, it is all for the best. In the first place, she never loved me. I have too high an opinion of her to suppose that if she had, she would have accepted you; in the second, she would never have married me against her mother's consent—and so, even if she had loved me, we should have both been miserable; and thirdly, if there is one thing that could console me under such a blow, it is, that the man she loves, and the family approve, is my dear old friend, who is far more worthy the happiness in store for him than I should have been." He put his hand kindly on my shoulder as his strong voice shook with the force of his suppressed emotion, and I bowed my head. I felt utterly humiliated by a magnanimity so noble, and by a tenderness surpassing that of women. I thanked God at that moment that Lady Ursula did *not* love me, and I vowed that Lady Broadhem should bitterly expiate her sins against us both. Here, then, was the secret of her refusing to acknowledge that she had stolen my missing letter at Dickiefield, and this was the precious use she had made of it. The question now was, What was to be done? But my mind was paralysed—all its strength seemed expended in vowing vengeance against Lady Broadhem. When I tried to form a sentence of explanation to Grandon, my brain refused its functions; I felt as if I were in a net, and that the slightest movement on my part would entangle me more inextricably in its meshes. The last resolution I had come to before he entered the room was on no account to tell him anything, and this resolution had now become an *idée fixe*. I had not clearness of mind at the moment to decide whether it was right or wrong. I felt that when my head was clear I had come to the conclusion that it was best, so I stuck to it now. True, it involved leaving him in the delusion that Ursula and I were engaged—but was it altogether certain to remain a delusion? Did Lady Ursula really care for him? I had only Lady Broadhem's word for it. Again, had I anything better to give him? would it be a comfort to him to hear the Chundango alternative? These in a confused way were the thoughts which flitted across my brain in this moment of doubt and difficulty, so I said nothing. He misinterpreted my silence, and thought me overwhelmed with remorse at the part I had played. "Believe me," he said, "I do not think one particle the worse of you for what you have done; I know how difficult it is to control one's feelings in moments of passion; and you see you were quite right not to believe Lady Broadhem when she told you Ursula cared for me."

"I had already written the letter," I stammered out.

"Of course you had: I never supposed you could do the dishonourable thing of hearing she cared about me first, and writing to her afterwards, although Lady Broadhem said so. When you did make the discovery that Lady Ursula's affections were not already engaged, you were perfectly right to win her if you could. I only bargain that you ask me to be your best man."

This was a well-meant but such a very unsuccessful attempt at resignation on Grandon's part, that it touched me to the quick. "My dear Grandon," I said—and I saw my face in the glass opposite, looking white and stony with the effort it cost me not to fall upon his neck and cry like a woman—"I solemnly swear, whatever you may think now, that the day will come when you will find that I was worthy the privilege of having been even your friend, I was going to say, Till then, believe me and trust me; but I need not, for I know that, however unnatural it seems for me to ask you not to allude again to the subject we have just been discussing, you will be satisfied that I would not ask it without having a reason which if you knew you would approve. On my conscience I believe that I am right in reserving from you my full confidence for the first time in my life; but do not let the fact of one forbidden topic alienate us—let it rather act as another link, hidden for the moment, but which may some day prove the most powerful to bind us together."

Grandon's face lit up with a bright frank smile. "I trust and believe in you from the bottom of my soul, and you shall bury any subject you like till it suits you to exhume it. Come, we will go to breakfast, and I will discourse to you on the political and military expediency of spending £200,000 on the fortifications of Quebec."

"Well," thought I, as I followed Grandon down-stairs, "for a man who is yearning to be honest, and to do the right thing by everybody, I have got into as elaborate a complication of lies as if I were a Russian diplomatist. First, I have given both Lady Broadhem and Grandon distinctly to understand that I am at this moment engaged to Ursula, which I am not; and secondly, I have solemnly assured that young lady herself that I am conscious of being occasionally mad."

In this tissue of falsehoods, it is poor consolation to think that the only one in which there may be some foundation of truth is the last. Supposing I was to go in for dishonesty, perhaps I could not help telling the truth by the rule of "contraries." I will go and ask the Honourable Spiffington whether he finds this to be the case, and I parted from Grandon in the hope of catching that gentleman before he had betaken himself to his civic haunts. I was too late, and pursued him east of Temple Bar. Here he frequented sundry "board-rooms" of companies which by a figure of speech he helped to "direct," and was also to be found in the neighbourhood of Hercules Passage and the narrow streets which surround the Stock Exchange, in the little back dens of pet brokers upon whom he relied for "good things." Spiffy used to collect political news in fashionable circles all through the night and up to an early hour of the morning, and then come into the City with it red-hot, so as to "operate." He was one of the most lively little rabbits to be found in all that big warren of which the Bank is the centre, and popped in and out of the different holes with a quickness that made him very difficult to catch. At last I ran him to a very dingy earth, where he was pausing, seated on a green baize table over a glass of sherry and a biscuit, and chaffing a rising young broker who hoped ultimately to be proposed by Spiffy for the Piccadilly Club. He was trying to establish a claim thereto now, on the strength of having been at Mrs Gorgon Tompkins's ball on the previous evening. "It is rather against you than otherwise," said Spiffy, who was an extremely off-hand little fellow, and did not interrupt his discourse after he had nodded to me familiarly; "I can't afford to take you up yet; indeed, what have you ever done to merit it? and Mrs Gorgon Tompkins has enough to do this season to keep her own head above water without attempting to float you. I did what I could for her last night, but she can't expect to go on with her successes of last year. We had a regular scene at

6 A.M. this morning, 'in banquet halls deserted'—tears, and all that sort of thing—nobody present but self, Gorgon, and partner. We took our last year's list, and compared them with the invitations sent out this year. The results were painful; only the fag-end of the diplomatic corps had responded—none of the great European powers present, and our own Cabinet most slenderly represented. Obliged to resort for young men to the byways and hedges; no expense spared, and yet the whole affair a miserable failure."

"Have you tried lobsters boiled in champagne at supper, as a draw?" said I.

"No," said Spiffy, looking at me with admiration; "I did not know this sort of thing was in your line, Frank." He had not the least right to call me Frank; but as everybody, whether they knew him or not, called him Spiffy, he always anticipated this description of familiarity.

"To tell you the truth, I could pull the Tompkinses through another season, but I am keeping all my best ideas for the Bodwinkles. Bodwinkles' first ball is to cost £2000. He wanted me to do it for £1500, and I should have been able to do it for that if Mrs Bodwinkle had had any *h*'s; but the *crême, de la crême* require an absence of aspirations to be made up to them somehow. Oh, with the extra £500 I can do it easily," said Spiffy, with an air of self-complacency. "She is a comparatively young woman, you see, without daughters; that simplifies matters very much. And then Bodwinkle can be so much more useful to political men than Gorgon Tompkins; the only fear is that he may commit himself at a late hour at the supper-table, but I have hit on a notion which will overcome all these possible *contretemps*."

"What is that?" said I, curiously.

"In confidence, I don't mind telling you, as you are not in the line yourself; but it is a master-stroke of genius. Like all great ideas, its merit lies in its simplicity."

"Don't keep us any longer in suspense; I promise not to appropriate it."

"Well," said Spiffy, triumphantly, "I am going to *pay* the aristocracy to come!"

"Pay them!" said I, really astounded; "how on earth are you going to get them to take the money?"

"Ah, that is the secret. Wait till the Bodwinkles' ball. You will see how delicately I shall contrive it; a great deal more neatly than you do when you leave your doctor's fee mysteriously wrapped in paper upon his mantelpiece. I shall no more hurt that high sense of honour, and that utter absence of anything like snobbism which characterises the best London Society, than a French cook would offend the nostrils of his guests with an overpowering odour of garlic; but it is a really grand idea."

"Worthy of Julius Cæsar, Charlemagne, or the first Napoleon," said I; "posterity will recognise you as a social giant with a mission, if the small men and the envious of the present day refuse to do so."

"I don't mind telling you," Spiffy went on, "that the idea first occurred to me in a Scotch donkey-circus, where I won, as a prize for entering the show, a red plush waistcoat worth five shillings. The fact is, Bodwinkle is so anxious to get people, he would go to any expense; he has even offered me a commission on all the accepted invitations I send out for him, graduated on a scale proportioned to the rank of the acceptor. I am afraid it would not be considered quite the right thing to take it; what do you think?"

"I doubt whether society would stand that. You must bring them to it gradually. At present, I feel sure they would draw the line at a 'commission.' Apropos of the Bodwinkles, I want to have a little private conversation with you."

"I am awfully done," said Spiffy. "I never went to bed at all last night. I got some information about Turkish certificates before I went to the Tompkinses; then I stayed there till past six, and had to come on here at ten to turn what I knew to account. However, go ahead; what is it in? Jones here will do it for you. No need of mystery between us. 'Cosmopolitan district' is the sort of thing I can conscientiously recommend—I'll tell you why: I went down to the lobby of the House last night on purpose to hear what the fellows were saying who prowl about there pushing what my wretched tailor would call 'a little bill' through Committee. It is becoming a sort of 'ring,' and the favourites last night were light Cosmopolitans."

"What on earth are they as distinguished from heavy?" I asked.

"Jones, show his lordship the stock-list," said Spiffy, with a swagger.

The investigation of the "list" completely bewildered me. Why a £10 share should be worth £19, and a £100 share worth £99, 10s., in the same company, was not evident on the face of the document before me, so I looked into Spiffy's.

"Puzzling, isn't it?" said Spiffy.

"Very," I replied. "Now tell me," and I turned innocently towards Mr Jones, for Spiffy's expression was secretive and mysterious—"explain to me how it is that a share upon which only £10 has been paid, should be so much more valuable than one which has been fully paid up."

"Ask the syndicate," said Jones, looking at Spiffy in a significant way.

I felt quite startled, for I expected to see a group of foreigners composing this institution walk into the room. It was not until I had looked again to Spiffy for information, and was met by the single open eye of that gentleman, that I drew an inference and a very long breath.

"Spiffy," I said, "I am getting stifled—the moral atmosphere of this place is tainted; take me to the sweetest board-room in the neighbourhood—I want to speak to you on private business."

"Haven't time," said Spiffy, looking at his watch.

"Not to settle little Lady Broadhem's little affair?" said I, in a whisper.

Spiffy got uncommonly pale, but recovered himself in a second. "All right, old fellow;" and he poured a few hurried words in an incomprehensible dialect into Jones's ear, and led the way to the Suburban Washing-ground Company's board-room, which was the most minute apartment of the kind I had ever seen.

I shall not enter into the particulars of what passed between Spiffy and myself on this occasion. In the first place, it is so dry that it would bore you; in the second place, it was so complicated, and Spiffy's explanations seemed to complicate it so much the more, that I could not make it clear to you if I wished; and, in the last, I do not feel justified in divulging all Lady Broadhem's money difficulties and private crises. Suffice it to say, that in the course of our conversation Spiffy was obliged to confide to me many curious facts connected with his own line of life, and more especially with the peculiar functions which he exercised in his capacity of a "syndic," under the seal of solemn secrecy. Without the hold over him which this little insight into his transactions has given me, I should not be able to report so much of our conversation as I have. Nevertheless I thought it right to tell him how much of it he would shortly see in print.

"Gracious, Frank," said Spiffy, petrified with alarm, "you don't mean to say you are going to publish all I told you about the Gorgon Tompkinses and the Bodwinkles? How am I ever to keep them going if you do? Besides, there are a number of other fellows in the same line as I am. Just conceive the injury you will inflict upon society generally—nobody will thank you. The rich 'middles' who are looking forward to this kind of advancement will be furious; all of us 'promoters' will hate you, and '*la haute*' will probably cut you. Why can't you keep quiet, instead of trying to get yourself and everybody else into hot water?"

"Spiffy," said I, solemnly, "when I devoted myself to 'mission work,' as they call it in Exeter Hall, I counted the cost, as you will see on referring back to my first chapter. I am still only at the beginning. I have a long and heavy task before me; but my only excuse for remaining in society is that I am labouring for its regeneration."

"You won't remain in it long," said Spiffy, "if you carry on in your present line. What do you want to do? Eradicate snobbism from the British breast?—never! We should all, from the highest to the lowest, perish of inanition without it."

"Society," said I, becoming metaphorical, "is like a fluid which is pervaded by that ingredient which you call 'snobbism,' the peculiarity of which is that you find it in equal perfection when it sinks to the bottom and becomes dregs, and when it rises to the surface and becomes *crême*—though of course it undergoes some curious chemical changes, according to its position. However, that is only one of the elements which pollute what should be a transparent fluid. I am subjecting it just now to a most minute and careful analysis, and I feel sure I shall succeed in obtaining an interesting 'precipitate.' I do most earnestly trust both you and the world at large will profit by my experiments."

"Frank, you are a lunatic," said Spiffy, with a yawn, for I was beginning to bore him. "I suppose I can't help your publishing what you like, only you will do yourself more harm than me. Let me know when society has 'precipitated' you out of it, and I will come and see you. Nobody else will. Good-bye!"

"He calls me a lunatic," I murmured, as I went downstairs; "I thought that I should be most likely to hear the truth by applying to the Honourable Spiffington."

The same reasons which have compelled me to maintain a certain reserve in relating my conversation with this gentleman prevent me fully describing the steps which I am at present taking to arrange Lady Broadhem's affairs, and which will occupy me during the Easter recess. Now, thank goodness, I think I see my way to preventing the grand crash which she feared, but I decline to state the amount of my own fortune which will be sacrificed in the operation. The great inconvenience of the whole proceeding is the secrecy which it necessarily involves. Grandon is under the impression that I am gambling on the Stock Exchange, and is miserable in consequence, because he fancies I add to that sin the more serious one of denying it. Lady Ursula, whom I have avoided seeing alone, but who knows that I am constantly plotting in secret with her mother, is no doubt beginning to think that I am wicked as well as mad, and is evidently divided between the secret obligation of keeping the secret of my insanity, and her dread lest in some way or other her mother should be the victim of it. Lady Bridget is unmistakably afraid of me. The other day when I went into the drawing-room and found her alone, she turned as pale as a sheet, jumped up, and stammered out something about going to find mamma, and rushed out of the room. Did I not believe in Ursula as in my own existence, I could almost fancy she had betrayed me. Then there is Broadhem. He is utterly puzzled. He knows that I am come to pull the family out of the mess, and put his own cherished little person into a financially sound condition; and he is equally well assured that I would not make this sacrifice without feeling certain of marrying his sister. But, in the first place, that any man should sacrifice anything, either for his sister or any other woman, is a mystery to Broadhem; and, in the second, I strongly suspect that Ursula has said something which makes him very doubtful whether she is engaged to me or not. Poor girl! I feel for her. Was ever a daughter and sister before placed in the embarrassing position of leaving her own mother and brother in the delusion that she was engaged to be married to a man who had never breathed to her the subject of his love, much less of matrimony? Then Spiffy and Lady Broadhem's lawyer both look upon the marriage as settled: how else can they account for the trouble I am taking, and the liberality I am displaying? There is something mysterious, moreover, in the terms upon which I am in the house. Lady Broadhem is beginning to think it unnatural that I should not care to see more of Ursula; and whenever she is not quite absorbed with considering her own affairs, is making the arrangement known among mammas by the expression, "bringing the young people together"—as if any young people who really cared to be together, could not bring themselves together without mamma or anybody else interfering. Fortunately Lady Broadhem is so much more taken up with her own speculations than with either her daughter's happiness or mine, that I am always able to give the conversation a City turn when she broaches the delicate subject of Ursula. How Ursula manages on these occasions I cannot conceive, but I do my best to prevent Lady Broadhem talking about me to her, as I always say mysteriously, that if she does, "it will spoil everything"—an alarming phrase, which produces an immediate effect. Still it is quite clear that this kind of thing can't continue long. If I can only keep matters going for a few days more, they will all be out of town for Easter, and that will give me time to breathe. As it is, it is impossible to shut my eyes to the fact, that my best friend is beginning to doubt me—that the girl I love dreads me—and that the rest of the family, and those sufficiently connected with it to observe my proceedings, either pity, laugh at, or despise me. This, however, by no means prevents their using their utmost endeavours to ruin me. That is the present state of matters. The situation cannot remain unchanged during the next four weeks. Have I your sympathies, dear reader? Do you wish me well out of it?

PART IV.
THE WORLD.
PICCADILLY, *May.*

The great difficulty which I find in this record of my eventful existence is, that I have too much to say. The sensations of my life will not distribute themselves properly. It is quite impossible for me to cram all that I think, say, and do every month into the limited space at my disposal. Thus I am positively overwhelmed with the brilliant dialogues, the elevating reflections, and the thrilling incidents, all of which I desire to relate. No one who has not tried this sort of thing can imagine the chronological, to say nothing of the crinological, difficulties in which I find myself. For instance, the incidents which occupied the whole of my last chapter took place in twenty-four hours, and yet how could I have left out either the poison-scene, or my interview with Grandon, or Spiffy's interesting social projects? Much better have left out the poison-scene, say some of my critical friends. It was not natural—too grotesque; but is that my fault? If nature has jammed me into a most unnatural and uncomfortable niche in that single step which is said to lead from the sublime to the ridiculous, am I responsible for it? If, instead of taking merely a serio-comic view of life, like some of my acquaintances, I regard it from a tragic-burlesque aspect, how can I help it? I did not put my ideas into my own head, nor invent the extraordinary things that happen to me,—and this is the reflection which renders me so profoundly indifferent to criticism. I shall have reviewers finding out that I am inconsistent with myself, and not true to nature here—as, for instance, when I fell violently in love with Ursula in one evening; or to the first principles of art there—as when I wrote to propose to her next morning: as if both art and nature could not take care of themselves without my bothering my head about them. Once for all, then, my difficulties do not arise from this source at all; they are, as I have said before, of the most simple character. In fact, they resolve themselves into Kant's two great *a priori* ideas, time and space. Now I could quite easily run on in the moral reflective vein to the end of the chapter, but then what should I do with the conversations which I ought to record, but to which I shall not be able to do justice, because I am so bound and fettered by the chain of my narrative? What an idea of weakness it conveys of an author who talks of "the thread of his narrative!" I even used to feel it when I was in the diplomatic service, and received a severe "wigging" once for writing in one of my despatches, "My lord, I have the honour to resume the 'tape' of my narrative"—so wedded is the Foreign Office to the traditions of its own peculiar style. I was glad afterwards they kept me to "the thread," as when I wanted finally to break it I found no difficulty. By the way, after I have done with society, I am going to take up the departments of the public service. If I let them alone just now, it is only because I am so desperately in love, and my love is so desperately hopeless; and the whole thing is in such a mess, that one mess is enough. At present I am setting my dwelling-house in order. When that is done I will go to work to clean out the "offices."

I may also allude here to another somewhat embarrassing circumstance which, had I not the good of my fellow-creatures at heart, might interfere with the progress of my narrative; and this is the morbid satisfaction which it seems to afford some people to claim for themselves the credit of being the most disagreeable or unworthy of those individuals with whom I am at present in contact. They would pretend, for instance, that there is no such person in society as Spiffington Goldtip, but that I mean him to represent some one else; and they take the 'Court Guide,' and find that no Lady Broadhem lives in Grosvenor Square, so they suppose that she too stands for some one else who does. Now, if I hear much of this sort of thing I shall stop altogether. In the first place, neither Spiffy nor Lady Broadhem will like it; and in the second, it is very disagreeable to me to be supposed to caricature my acquaintances under false names. The cap is made a great deal too large to fit any particular individual, so there is no use in trying it on; but when, perchance, I find groups of people acting unworthily, I should be falling into the same error for which I blame the parsonic body of the present day, if I shrank from exposing and cutting straight into the sores that they are fain to plaster and conceal. In these days of amateur preaching in theatres and other unconsecrated buildings, I feel I owe no apology to my clerical brethren for taking their congregations in hand after they have quite done with them.

People may call me a "physician" or any other name they like, and tell me to heal myself; but it is quite clear that a sick physician who needs rest, and yet devotes all his time and energies to the curing of his neighbours, is a far more unselfish individual than one who waits to do it till he is robust. Therefore, if I am caught doing myself the very things I find fault with in others, "that has nothing at all to do with it," as Lady Broadhem always says when all her arguments are exhausted.

Those of my readers who have taken an interest in her ladyship's speculations and in my endeavours to extricate her from her pecuniary embarrassments, may conceive our feelings upon hearing of the surrender of General Lee. I regret to say that, in spite of every device which the experience of Spiffy, of Lady Broadhem's lawyer, and of Lady B. herself could suggest, her liabilities have increased to such an extent in consequence of the rapid fall of Confederate stock, that I was obliged to take advantage of the Easter recess to run over to Ireland to make arrangements for selling an extremely encumbered estate which I purchased as a speculation some years ago, but have never before visited. This trip has given me an opportunity of enabling me thoroughly to master the Irish question. I need scarcely say how much I was surprised at the prosperous condition of the peasants of Connemara after the accounts I had received of them. When I "surveyed" my own estate, which consists of seven miles of uninterrupted rock, I regarded with admiration the population who could find the means of subsistence upon it, and whose rags were frequently of a very superior quality. I also felt how creditable it was to the British Government, that by a judicious system of legislation it should succeed in keeping people comparatively happy and contented, whose principal occupation seemed to me to consist in wading about the sea-beach looking for sea-weed, and whose diet was composed of what they found there. That every Irishman I met should expect me to lament with him the decrease by emigration in the population of a nation which subsists chiefly on peat and periwinkles, illustrated in a striking manner the indifference which the individuals of this singular race have for each other's sufferings; and it is quite a mistake, therefore, to suppose that absentee landlords, who are for the most part Irish, live away from their properties because they are so susceptible to the sight of distress that they cannot bear to look upon their own tenantry. To an Englishman nothing is more consoling than to feel that the Irish question is essentially an Irish question, and that Englishmen have nothing at all to do with it—that the tenant-right question is one between Irish landlords and Irish tenants—that the religious question is one between Irish Catholics and Irish Protestants—and that the reason that no Englishman can understand them is, because they are Irish, and inverted brains would be necessary to their comprehension. These considerations impressed themselves forcibly upon my notice at a meeting of the National League, which I attended in Dublin, the object of which was to secure the national independence of Ireland, and to free it from the tyranny of British rule. One of the speakers made out so strong a case for England, that I could only account for it by the fact that he was an Irishman arguing the case of his own country. "How," he asked, "is the English Parliament to know our grievances, when out of 105 members that we send up to it, there are not two who are honest? Why is not the O'Donoghue in the chair to-day? he is the only real patriot, and we can't trust him. Why are the Irish Protestants not true to themselves and the cause? Why, in fact, is there not a single man of the smallest position and influence either on the platform or in the body of the house, except myself, who am a magistrate of the county of Cork, and therefore unable to advocate those violent measures by which alone our liberties are to be gained? Is it because we have got them already? No; but because Irishmen do not care a farthing about them. Shame on them for their apathy," &c. It was pleasant to listen to this Irish patriot inveighing against his countrymen, and finally making England responsible for Irishmen being what they are. Bless them! my heart warmed towards them as I saw them at Queenstown trooping on board an emigrant-ship, looking ruddy and prosperous, bound on the useful errand of propagating Fenianism, of exhibiting themselves as choice specimens of an oppressed nationality, and of devoting their brilliant political instincts, their indefatigable industry, and their judicial calmness, to the service of that country which is at present in danger of suffering from a determination of blood to the head in the person of Andy Johnson. If anything can trim that somewhat crank craft "United States," let us hope that it will be by taking in Irishmen at the rate of one thousand per week to serve as ballast; for most certainly the best means of increasing the sailing qualities of the leaky old tub, "British Constitution," will be by inducing the ballast aforesaid to throw itself overboard. I was pitching and rolling abominably between Kingston and Holyhead as I drew this appropriate nautical parallel, and was not in a mood to relish the following announcement, which appeared in the pages of a fashionable organ, that happened to be the first journal I bought in England:—

"We are in a position to state that a marriage is arranged between Lord Frank Vanecourt, M.P., second son of the late Duke of Dunderhead, and Lady Ursula Newlyte, eldest daughter of the late Earl of Broadhem."

How I envied "our position," and what a very different one mine was! However, the notice served its purpose, for it prepared me for what I should have to encounter in London—the sort of running fire of congratulation I must expect to undergo all along Piccadilly, down St James's Street, and along Pall Mall. Should I simper a coy admission, or storm out an indignant denial? On the whole, the most judicious line seemed to be to do each alternately. The prospect of puzzling the gossip-mongers generally almost consoled me for the feeling of extreme annoyance which I had experienced. "The imbroglio must clear itself at last," thought I, "but it will be a curious amusement to see how long I can keep it from doing so;" and I bought an evening paper as I approached London, by way of distracting my mind. The first news which thrilled me as I opened it was the announcement of the assassination of President Lincoln. I am not going to moralise on this event now, and only allude to it as it affects the story of my own life. It saved me that evening from the embarrassment I had anticipated; for even when I went to the Cosmopolitan, I found everybody listening to Mr Wog, so that nobody cared about my private affairs, and it induced Lady Broadhem to make a secret expedition into the City of a speculative nature next morning, as I accidentally discovered from Spiffy. It is not impossible that the knowledge of this breach of faith on her part may prove a valuable piece of information to me.

I sauntered into "the Piccadilly" on the following afternoon, armed at all points, and approached the bay-window, in which I observed Broadhem and several others seated round the table, with the utmost *insouciance*. They had evidently just talked my matter over, for my appearance caused a momentary pause, and then a general chorus of greeting. Broadhem, with an air of charming *naïveté* and brotherly regard, almost rushed into my arms; but his presence restrained that general expression of frank opinion on the part of the rest of the company, with reference to my luck, with which the fortunate *fiancé* is generally greeted. Still, the characters of my different so-called "friends," and their forms of congratulation, were amusing to watch. There was the patronising, rather elderly style—"My dear Vanecourt, I can't tell you how happy the news has made me. I was just saying to Broadhem,"—and so on; then the free and easy "Frank, old fellow" and "slap on the back" style; then the "knowing shot" and "poke in the ribs" style; then the "feelings too much for me" style—severe pressure of the hands, and silence, accompanied by upturned eyes; then the "serious change of state and heavy responsibilities" style. Oh, I know them all, and am thankful to say the peculiar versatility of my talents enabled me to give as many different answers as there are styles. I am not such a fool as not to know exactly what all my friends said of the match behind my back: "Sharp old woman, Lady Broadhem; she'll make that flat, Frank Vanecourt, pay all the Broadhem debts;" or, "Odd thing it is that such a nice girl as Ursula Newlyte should throw herself away on such a maniac as Frank Vanecourt;" then, "Oh, she'd marry anybody to get away from such a mother;" again, "I always thought Vanecourt a fool, but I never supposed he would have deliberately submitted to be bled by the Broadhems." That is the sort of thing that will go on with variations in every drawing-room in London for the next few evenings. Now I am striking out quite a new line to meet the humbug, the hypocrisy, the scandal, and the ill-nature of which both Ursula and myself are the subjects. Thus, when Broadhem greeted me in the presence of the company, after I had received their congratulations with a good deal of ambiguous embarrassment, I appeared to be a little overcome, and, linking my arm in that of my future brother-in-law, walked him out of the room. "My dear Broadhem," said I, "for reasons which it is not necessary for me now to enter into, but which are connected with the pecuniary arrangements I am making to put your family matters straight, this announcement is a most unfortunate occurrence—we must take measures to contradict it immediately."

"Why," said Broadhem, "if it is the case, as you know it is, I don't see the harm of announcing it. To tell you the truth, I think it ought to have been announced sooner, and that you have been putting Ursula lately in rather a false position, by seeming to avoid her so much in society, because, you know, it has been talked of for some time past."

"Ah, then, I fancy the announcement was made on your authority," I said. "It is a pity, as I had made up my mind to postpone the ceremony until I had not only completed all my arrangements for putting your family matters square, but could actually see my way towards gradually clearing off the more pressing liabilities with which the estate is encumbered. You know what a crotchety fellow I am. Now, my plan is, clear everything off first, and marry afterwards; and unless you positively contradict the report of my marriage with your sister, I shall immediately countermand the instructions under which my lawyers are acting, and take no further steps whatever in the matter." I felt a malicious pleasure in watching Broadhem's face during this speech, as I was sure that he had done his best to spread the report of my marriage with his sister for fear of my backing out, and escaping from my obligations in respect to his financial embarrassments. It is only fair to him to state, that these were none of his own creating—he had been a perfect model of steadiness all his life. "It will be pleasanter for us both," I went on, "that the world should never be able to say, after my marriage with your sister, that you and your mother continue to live upon us. Now, I tell you fairly, that, for family reasons, this premature announcement renders it impossible for me to proceed with those arrangements which must precede my connection with your family."

Broadhem's face grew very long while he listened to this speech. "But," he said, "it is not fair to Ursula that everybody should suppose that you are engaged to her, and refuse to acknowledge it."

"Pray, whose fault is it," said I, "that anybody supposes anything about it? I have never told a soul that I was engaged to be married, and if you and your mother choose to go spreading unauthorised reports, you must take the consequences; but"—and a sudden inspiration flashed upon me—"I will tell you what I will do, I will be guided entirely by Lady Ursula's wishes in the matter. If she wishes the report contradicted, I must insist most peremptorily on both Lady Broadhem and yourself taking the necessary steps to stop the public gossip; but if she is willing that the marriage should be announced, I pledge you my word that I will allow no preconceived plans to influence me, or pecuniary difficulties to stand in the way, but will do whatever she, your mother, and yourself wish."

"Very well," said Broadhem, "that sounds fair enough. I'll go and see Ursula at once."

"Not quite so fast; please take me with you," I said. "As it is a matter most closely affecting my future happiness, I must be present at the interview, and so must Lady Broadhem."

"I don't think that is an arrangement which will suit Ursula at all. In fact, both she and my mother are so incomprehensible and mysterious, that I am sure they will object to any such meeting. Whenever I have spoken to my mother about it, she always meets me with, 'For goodness' sake, don't breathe a word to Ursula, or you will spoil all;' and when, in defiance of this injunction, I did speak to Ursula, she said, in a lackadaisical way, that she had no intention of marrying any one at present; and when I went on to say that in that case she had no business to accept you, she asked me what reason I had for supposing that she ever had done so; and when I said, 'the assurance of my mother's ears in the drawing-room at Dickiefield,' she stared at me with amazement, and burst into a flood of tears."

"Under these circumstances, don't you think you would have done better not to meddle in the matter at all?" I remarked. "However, the mischief is done now, and perhaps the best plan will be for you to bring about a meeting between your sister and myself. I suppose whatever we arrange will satisfy you and Lady Broadhem?"

"Well, I don't know," said Broadhem, doubtfully; "she does not seem to know her own mind, and I don't feel very sure of you. However, you are master of the situation, and can arrange what you like. My mother is going to a May meeting at Exeter Hall to-morrow to hear Caribbee Islands and Chundango hold forth. I know the latter is to call for her at eleven, so if you will come at half-past, I will take care that you have an opportunity of seeing Ursula alone."

This conversation took place as we were strolling arm-in-arm down St James's Street on our way to the House, thereby enabling the groups of our friends who inspected us from divers club-windows to assert confidently the truth of the report.

Just as I was parting from Broadhem at the door of the lobby we were accosted suddenly by Grandon. He looked very pale as he grasped my hand and nodded to my companion, who walked off towards "another place" without waiting for a further greeting. "I suppose, now that your marriage is publicly announced, Frank, it need no longer be a tabooed subject between us, and that you will receive my congratulations."

My first impulse was to assure him that the announcement was unauthorised so far as I was concerned, but the prospect of the impending interview with Ursula restrained me, and I felt completely at a loss. "Don't you think, Grandon," I said, "that I should have told you as much as gossip tells the public, had I felt myself entitled to do so? I only ask you to trust me for another twenty-four hours, and I will tell you everything."

Grandon looked stern. "You are bound not to allow the report to go one moment uncontradicted if there is nothing in it; and if there is, you are now equally bound to acknowledge it."

"Surely," I said, in rather a piqued tone, "Broadhem is as much interested in the matter as you are, and he is satisfied with my conduct."

"I tell you fairly I am not," said Grandon. "You will do Lady Ursula a great injustice, and yourself a great injury, if you persist in a course which is distinctly dishonourable."

At that moment who should come swaggering across the lobby where we happened to be standing but Larkington and Dick Helter! "Well, Frank, when is it to be?" said the latter. "You were determined to take the world by surprise, and I must congratulate you on your success."

"Thanks," said I, calmly, for I was smarting under Grandon's last words: "the day is not yet fixed. What between Lady Broadhem's scruples about Lent and some arrangements I had to make in Ireland, there has been a good deal of delay, but I think," I went on, with a slight simper, "that it has nearly come to an end."

"There," said I to Grandon, when they had favoured me with a few *banalités*, and passed on, "that is explicit enough, surely; will that satisfy you, or do you like this style better?" and I turned to receive Bower and Scraper, who generally hunt tufts and scandal in couples, and were advancing towards us with much *empressement*.

"My dear Lord Frank, charmed to see you; no wonder you are looking beaming, for you are the luckiest man in London," said Bower.

"How so?" said I, looking unconscious.

"Come, come," said Scraper, and he winked at me respectfully; "we have known all about it for the last two months. I got it out of Lord Broadhem very early in the day."

"Then you got a most deliberate and atrocious fabrication, for I suppose you mean the report of my marriage to his sister, and I beg you will contradict it most emphatically whenever you hear it," said I, very stiffly. And I walked on into the House, leaving Grandon more petrified than the two little toadies I had snubbed. I can generally listen to Gladstone when he is engaged in keeping the House in suspense over the results of his arithmetical calculations; but the relative merits of a reduction of the tax on tea and on malt fell flat on my ears that evening, and even the consideration of twopence in the pound off the income-tax failed to exercise that soothing influence on my mind which it seemed to produce on those around. I looked in vain for Grandon; his accustomed seat remained empty, and I felt deeply penitent and miserable. What is there in my nature that prompts me, when I am trying to act honestly and nobly, to be impracticable and perverse? Grandon could not know the extent of the complication in which I am involved, and was right in saying what he did; yet I could no more at the moment help resenting it as I did, than a man in a passion who is struck can help returning the blow. Then the fertility and readiness of invention which the demon of perverseness that haunts me invariably displays, fairly puzzles me. And you too, I thought, as I looked up and saw little Scraper whispering eagerly to Dick Helter, who was regarding me with a bewildered look, quite unconscious that the Chancellor of the Exchequer had become poetical in regard to rags, and was announcing that we were about

"To serve as model for the mighty world,And be the fair beginning of a time,"

—"ah," thought I, as I gazed on that brilliant and ingenious orator, "he is the only man in the House, who, if he was in such a mess as I am, would find a way out of it."

My first impulse on the following morning, before going to Grosvenor Square, was to go and apologise to Grandon; and I had an additional reason for doing so after reading the following paragraph in the 'Morning Post':—

"The Earl and Countess of Whitechapel had the honour of entertaining at dinner last night the Marquess and Marchioness of Scilly, the Countess (Dowager) of Broadhem, the Earl of Broadhem and Lady Ursula Newlyte, Mr and Lady Jane Helter, Lord Grandon, the Honourable Spiffington Goldtip, and Mr Scraper."

To have made it thoroughly unlucky I ought to have been there as a thirteenth. As it is, I wonder what conclusion the company in general arrived at in reference to the affair in which I am so nearly interested, and I told them off in the order in which they must have gone in to dinner. The Scillys and Whitechapels paired off; Helter took down old Lady Broadhem; Broadhem took Lady Jane; Grandon, Lady Ursula; and Spiffy and Scraper brought up the rear. I pictured the delight with which Helter would mystify Lady Broadhem, by allowing her to extract from him what he had heard first from me and then from Scraper, and how Spiffy and Scraper would each pretend to have the right version of the story, and be best informed on this important matter. All this was easy enough, but my imagination failed to suggest what probably passed between Grandon and Ursula; so I screwed up my courage and determined to go up to Grandon's room and find out We often used to breakfast together, and I sent up my servant to tell him to expect me. Under the circumstances I thought it right to give him the opportunity of refusing to see me, but I knew him too well to think that he would take advantage of it.

He was sitting at his writing-table looking pale and haggard, as I entered, and turned wearily towards me with an air of reserve very foreign to his nature.

"My dear Grandon," I said, "I have come to apologise to you for my unjustifiable conduct yesterday, but you cannot conceive the worry and annoyance to which I have been subject by the impertinent curiosity and unwarrantable interference of the world in my private affairs. When you told me I was acting dishonourably, an impulse of petulance made me forget what was due to Ursula, and answer my inquisitive friends as I did; but I am on my way to Grosvenor Square now, and will put matters straight in an hour."

"The mischief is done," said Grandon, gloomily, "and it is not in your power to undo it. Whatever may have been the motives by which you have been actuated—and far be it from me to judge them—you have caused an amount of misery which must last as long as those whom you have chosen as your victims live."

"I beseech you be more explicit," I said; "what happened last night?—I insist upon knowing."

"You know perfectly well that as you stand in no nearer relation to Lady Ursula than I do," and Grandon's voice trembled, while his eye gleamed for a second with a flash of triumph, "you have no right to insist upon anything; but I have no objection to tell you that as Lady Ursula was quite in ignorance of any such report having currency as that which has now received a certain stamp of authority, by virtue of the conspiracy into which you seem to have entered with her mother and brother, she was overwhelmed with confusion at the congratulations which it seems the ladies heaped upon her after dinner last night, and finally fainted. Of course all London will be talking of it to-day, as the Helters went away early on purpose to get to Lady Mundane's before Scraper could arrive there with his version of the catastrophe."

"Did she tell you she did not care for me, Grandon?" said I, very humbly.

"She told me to forgive you, and love you as I used to, God help me!" burst out Grandon, and he covered his face with his hands. "Frank," he said, "she is an angel of whom neither you nor I is worthy; but oh, spare her! Don't, for God's sake hold her up to the pity and curiosity of London. I would do anything on earth she told me; but what spell have you thrown over her that in spite of your heartless conduct she should still implore me to love and cherish you? How can I obey her in this when your acts are so utterly at variance with all that is noble and honourable? I have at least one cause for gratitude," he continued, in a calmer tone, "and that is, that the doubt which would force itself upon me when I vainly tried to account for her conduct in accepting you so suddenly has been removed."

I had discovered what I wanted, for in spite of every effort to conceal it, I detected a mixture of jealousy and of triumph in Grandon's last speech. Ursula, in her moment of agony, had unconsciously allowed him to perceive that he alone was loved, and had urged him still to love and cherish me, because as an irresponsible being she had thought me more than ever in need of sympathy and protection For a moment I wavered in my resolution. Should I open my heart and give my dearest friend a confidence which should justify me in his eyes, at the risk of destroying the project I had formed on that night when, walking home from my interview with Lady Broadhem, I had determined to devote my energies to the happiness of others and not of myself? or should I maintain that flippant, heartless exterior which seemed for the time necessary to the success of my plans? As usual, my mind made itself up while I was doubting what to do, and in spite of myself I said jauntily, "Well, now that you know that she cares about you and not about me, I suppose you have nothing to do but to return her affection?"

"I have done that for some time," he replied, "but you know how perfectly hopeless our love is; and yet," and his voice deepened and his face flushed with enthusiasm, "I am happier loving hopelessly and knowing that I am loved, than I have ever been before. Forgive me, Frank, but I do not feel for you as I should have done had you behaved differently. You had no right to let me suppose that she had accepted you when the subject had never been breathed between you. Your conscience must tell you that you have acted in an unworthy manner towards us both."

"Grandon," I said, sententiously, "my conscience works on a system utterly incomprehensible to an ordinary intelligence, and I am quite satisfied with it. I will have a metaphysical discussion with you on the matter on some other occasion. Meantime you think Ursula has decided on preferring the ruin and disgrace of the Broadhem family to a *mariage de convenance* either with me or any one else?"

"I did not know it was a question of disgrace," said Grandon, "and I am quite sure that Lady Ursula will do the right thing. I would rather not discuss the subject any further; we shall certainly not agree, and I am afraid that we might become more widely estranged than I should wish. Here is breakfast. It was you who last asked me to bury this unhappy subject, it is my turn now to make the same request. I wish to heaven it had never arisen between us."

"What a lucky fellow you are!" said I, looking at him with the eye of a philosopher; "now you would never imagine yourself to be one of the most enviable men in London, with the most charming of women and the most devoted of friends ready to sacrifice themselves at your feet—she *incomprise*, I *incompris*."

"Don't trifle," said Grandon, sternly, interrupting me; "my patience is not inexhaustible."

"Luckily mine is," said I, with my mouth full of grilled salmon, "otherwise I should not be the right stuff for a social missionary. Apropos, you have never asked me what I have been doing in that line; nor told me what you thought of the long letter I wrote you from Flityville. Did you get me the answers to those questions?"

"No," he replied, "I must honestly tell you, Frank, that it pains me to discuss so serious a subject with one who makes so fair and earnest a pretence of having deep convictions as you do, and whose acts are so diametrically opposed to them; and now I must be off, for I have a committee of the House to attend."

"And I a rendezvous of a still more interesting character to keep;" and as I left Grandon I observed a shade of disgust and disappointment cross his face at my last speech. I always overdo it, I thought, as I walked towards Grosvenor Square, but Grandon ought to make allowances for me. He has known me all my life, but it was reserved for us both to be in love with the same woman to bring out the strong points in each of us. Lavater says you never know whether a man is your friend until you have divided an inheritance with him; but it is a much more ticklish thing to go halves in a woman's love. Never mind, I will astonish them both yet. Now then, to begin with her; and I boldly knocked at the door. I found Broadhem in his own little den.

"It is all right," he said, as I entered; "I have told Ursula you are coming, and she will see you in the drawing-room."

I had not been for two minutes alone with Lady Ursula since we parted at Dickiefield; indeed, when it is remembered that my whole intercourse with her upon that occasion extended over little more than twenty-four hours, and that we had never been on any other terms since than those of the most casual acquaintances, the embarrassing nature of the impending interview presented itself to me in a somewhat unpleasant aspect. Now that it had come to the point, I could not make up my mind exactly what to say. I tried to collect my ideas and go over the history of the events which had resulted in the present predicament. Why was I in the singular position of having to make a special appointment with a young lady with whom I was desperately in love, whom I knew but slightly, but who supposed me to be mad, for the purpose of asking her, first, whether she considered herself engaged to be married to me or not; and secondly, if not, whether she would have any objection to the world supposing that such was the case? Now my readers will remember that the sudden impulse which induced me in the first instance to delude Lady Broadhem into believing that Lady Ursula had accepted me, arose from the desire to save her from the tender mercies of Chundango. Lady Ursula had in fact owed the repose she had enjoyed for the last two months entirely to her supposed engagement to me. The moment that is at an end, her fate becomes miserable. If she will but consider herself drowning, and me the straw, I shall only be too happy to be clutched. If I cannot propose myself as a husband, I will at least suggest that she should regard me in the light of a straw.

I had got thus far when I found myself in her presence. She looked very pale, and there was an expression of decision about the corners of her mouth which I had not before remarked. It did not detract from its sweetness, nor did the slight tremor of the upper lip as she greeted me detract from its force. It is a great mistake to suppose that a tremor of the lip denotes weakness; on the contrary, it often arises from a concentration of nervous energy. I am not quite so sure about a tremor of the knees. That was what I suffered from at the moment, together with a very considerable palpitation of the heart. Now the difficulty at such a moment is to know how to begin. I have often heard men say that when they have obtained an interview with a great statesman for the purpose of asking a favour, and he waits for them to begin without helping them out with a word, they have experienced this difficulty. That arises from the consciousness that they are sacrificing their self-respect to their "career." If they would never go near a statesman except when they wanted to confer a favour upon him, they would have no difficulty in finding words. Fortunately the great majority of our public *employés* are not yet hardened beggars like the Neapolitans, and are not, like them, dead to any sentiment of shame upon these occasions, though it is to be feared that they will soon become so. The responsibility of demoralising the servants of the public lies entirely with the heads of the departments. In proportion as these gentlemen are not ashamed of sacrificing their subordinates in order to keep themselves in office, will those subordinates become as unblushing place-hunters as their masters are place-keepers. Once accustom a man to being a scapegoat, and you destroy at a blow his respect for himself and for the man who offers him up. I could become very eloquent upon this subject, if I was not afraid of keeping Ursula waiting. There are few men who need having their duties pointed out to them more constantly than Cabinet Ministers. Attacks in the House of Commons do them no good, as they are generally the result of party tactics, and spring from as unworthy a motive as does the defence. Men who have got place do not pay much attention to attacks from men who want it. Then, as I said before, the Church utterly ignores its duties in this respect. Who ever heard of a bishop getting up and pointing out to her Majesty's Ministers the necessity of considering the interests of the country before their own? It would be immediately supposed that he was bullying them, because he wanted to be "translated;" and this would be considered the only excuse for the same want of "good taste" which I, who am only desirous for their good, am now displaying. I put it to you, my lords, in all humility, do you ever get up in your places, not in the House of Peers, but in another House, and point out to the rulers of the country that no personal consideration should ever interfere with their doing the right thing at the right moment? Do you ever explain to the noble lords among whom you sit, that when a committee is chosen from both sides of the House to inquire into a simple question of right or wrong, the members of it are bound to vote upon its merits and according to their consciences, rather than according to the political parties to which they belong? and do you ever ask yourselves what you would do in the same circumstances? Do you ever tell the heads of departments that they are responsible for the *morale* which pervades the special services over which they preside? that the tone of honour, the amount of zeal and of disinterestedness which subordinates display must depend in a great measure upon the example set them by their chief? that you can no more expect an orchestra to play in tune with a leader devoid of a soul for music, than a department to work well without the soul of honour at its head? Do you ever tell the leaders of the party with which you "act" that it is wicked openly to collect funds to give candidates to bribe with at general elections? Do you ever faithfully tell these great men, that just in proportion as their position is elevated, so is their power for good or for evil? and when you see their responsibilities sit lightly upon them, do you ever take them to task for trifling with the highest interests of the country, and stifling the consciences of its servants? If the fact that in your ecclesiastical capacity you are beholden to one or other of the political parties makes it delicate for you to attack your opponents, then let the Liberal Episcopacy jealously guard the honour of the Liberal Cabinets, and the Tory bishops watch over the public morality of their own side so soon as it shall come into office.

Of course I was not thinking of all this as I entered the drawing-room, but I had thought it often before, and feel impelled to mention it now. What I actually did was to blush a good deal, stammer a good deal, and finally make the unpleasant discovery that that presence of mind which my readers will ere this have perceived I possess to an eminent degree, had entirely deserted me. I think this arose from the extreme desire I felt that Lady Ursula should not at that moment imagine that I was mad. Perhaps, my reader, it may have happened to you to have to broach the most delicate of all topics to a young lady who regarded you in the light of a rather dangerous lunatic, and you can therefore enter into my feelings. I was not sorry to find myself blushing and stammering, as it might have the effect of reassuring her, and making her feel that for the moment at least I was quite harmless.

"I am glad, Lord Frank," she said, observing my confusion, "that you have given me this opportunity of seeing you, as I am sure you would not willingly inflict pain, and should you find that you have unintentionally done so, will make all the reparation in your power."

At this moment I glanced significantly at Broadhem, who left the room.

"Unfortunately it too often happens, Lady Ursula," I said, "that it is necessary to inflict a temporary pain to avert what might become a permanent misery."

"I cannot conceive," replied she, "to what permanent misery, as affecting myself, you can allude, in which your intervention should be necessary, more especially when exhibited in a form which places me in such a false position. I need not say that the announcement which I saw for the first time in a newspaper caused me the greatest annoyance; but when I found afterwards that my mother, my brother, and even Lord Grandon, had heard it from your own lips many weeks before, and that in fact you had given my mother, under a promise that she would not allude to the subject to me, such a totally erroneous idea of what passed at our interview at Dickiefield,—when I thought of all this, I could only account for it by the last revelation you made to me there."

She maintained her self-possession perfectly until she was obliged to allude to my insanity, then she dropped her eyelids, and the colour for the first time rushed into her cheeks as she shrank from touching on this delicate subject. At the moment I almost felt inclined to tell her that I was as sane as she was, but refrained, partly because I was not sure of it myself, partly because I did not think she would believe me, partly because, after all, it might be the best justification I could offer for my conduct, and partly because I was not quite ready to enter upon an explanation of the ruse by which I had hoped to save her from the persecution of her mother to marry Chundango. This suddenly reminded me of my idea that she was in the position of one drowning. I therefore said, in a careless way, for the purpose of showing her that her allusion to my insanity had produced no unfavourable impression upon me,——

"Lady Ursula, would you have any objection to regarding me in the light of a straw?"

"A what!" said Lady Ursula, in a tone in which amazement seemed blended with alarm.

"A straw," I repeated; "I assure you you are drowning, and even an unworthy being like myself may be of use to you, if you would but believe it. Remember Chundango's conduct at Dickiefield—remember the view Lady Broadhem took of it, until I interposed, or as I should more accurately say, until the current swept me past her—remember that up to this moment she has never recurred to the subject of Mr Chundango, who, although he comes to the house constantly, now devotes himself entirely to Lady Broadhem herself; and, allow me to say it, you owe it all to a timely straw."

Lady Ursula seemed struck by the graphic way in which I put her position before her, and remained silent for a few moments. It had evidently never occurred to her, that I had indirectly been the means of securing her tranquillity. She little thought it possible that her mother could have talked her matrimonial prospects over with a comparative stranger in the mercantile terms which Lady Broadhem had used in our interview at Dickiefield. And I am well aware that society generally would consider such conduct on the part of her ladyship coarse and unladylike. It showed a disregard of *les convenances* which good society is the first to resent. Those who have never secretly harboured the designs which Lady Broadhem in the agony of a financial crisis avowed, might justly repudiate her conduct; but "conscience does make cowards of us all," and fashionable mothers will naturally be the first to censure in Lady Broadhem a practice to which, in a less glaring and obnoxious form, they are so strongly addicted. If in silvery accents she had confided her projects to Lady Mundane, the world would have considered it natural and ladylike enough; the coarseness consisted in her telling them to me. O generation of slave-owners! why persist in deluding yourselves into the belief, that so long as you buy and sell your own flesh and blood in a whisper there is no harm in it?

My gentle critics, I would strongly advise you not to place me on my defence in these matters; I have every disposition to let you down as gently as possible, but if you play tricks with the rope, I shall have to let you down by the run. Why, it was only last year that all the world went to Mrs Gorgon Tompkins's second ball. They no more cared than she did, that she had lost one of her daughters early in the season, just after she had given the first. I remember Spiffy Goldtip taking public opinion in the club about it, and asking whether an interval of four months was not enough to satisfy the requirements of society in the matter, as it would be so sad if, after having made such good social running before Easter, Mrs Gorgon Tompkins were to lose it all afterwards through an unfortunate domestic *contretemps* of this kind. Now I doubt whether Lady Broadhem could surpass that. However, she is capable of great feats, and I fully expect she will strike out a new line soon; there has been a lurking demon in her eye of late which alarms me. Fortunately I am not yet finally committed, financially. It is true it has cost me a few thousands, which I shall never see again, to tide the family over its difficulties thus far, but I can still let it down with a crash if it suits me.

"Lord Frank," said Lady Ursula, after a pause, "I have already alluded to the circumstance which has induced me to treat you with a forbearance which I could not have extended to one whom I regarded as responsible for conduct unwarrantable towards myself, and certainly not to be justified by any possible advantage which I might be supposed to derive from it. I consented to see you now, because I feel sure that when you know from my own lips that I wish you at once to deny the rumour you have been the means of originating, I may depend upon your doing so."

"May I ask," I said, with much contrition in my tone, "what explanation you gave Lady Broadhem on the subject?"

"If you mean," said Lady Ursula, "whether I accounted to mamma for your conduct as I do to myself—in other words, whether I betrayed your secret—I have carefully refrained from discussing the subject with her. Fortunately, after dinner at the Whitechapels' last night, Broadhem told me that he had seen you, and that you were coming here to-day, so I assured mamma that she would hear from you the true state of the case; though, of course, I felt myself bound to let her understand that, owing to a fact which I was unable to explain, she had been completely misled by you."

"And what did Lady Broadhem say?" I asked.

"She said that had it not been for a meeting she was obliged to attend this morning, she would have waited to see you to-day; but that she was sure I laboured under some strange delusion, and that a few words of explanation from you would smooth everything."

"Will you allow me to tell you what those few words are?" said I. "Lady Broadhem little imagines the real state of the case, because she knows what you do not know, that I am engaged in clearing off her own pecuniary liabilities, and making arrangements by which the old-standing claims on the Broadhem estates may be met. You may never have heard how seriously the family is embarrassed, and how unlucky all Lady Broadhem's attempts to retrieve its fortunes by speculation have been. I could only account to her for the pecuniary sacrifices she knows I am making by allowing her to suppose that I was incurring them for your sake." I could not resist letting a certain tone of pique penetrate this speech, and the puzzled and pained expression of Lady Ursula's face afforded me a sense of momentary gratification, of which I speedily repented. As she looked at me earnestly, her large blue eyes filled slowly with tears. "Is she crying because this last speech of mine proves me hopelessly mad?" thought I; "or does she feel herself in a pecuniary trap, and is she crying because she does not see her way out of it?" and I felt the old sensation coming over me, and my head beginning to swim. Why, oh why, am I denied that method in my madness which it must be such a comfort to possess? It is just at the critical moment that my osseous matter invariably plays me a trick. I seemed groping for light and strength, and mechanically put out my hand; the soft touch of one placed gently in it thrilled through my nerves with an indescribable current, and instantaneously the horrid feeling left me, and I emerged from the momentary torpor into which I had fallen. I don't think Ursula remarked it, for she said, and her eyes were now overflowing, in a voice of surpassing sweetness, "Lord Frank, I have discovered your *real* secret; it is no longer possible for you to conceal the noble motives which have actuated you under your pretended——"

"Hush!" I said, interrupting her; "what I did, whether rightly or wrongly, I did for the best. Now I will be guided by your wishes. What am I to do?"

"Allow no worldly consideration, however unselfish, either for myself or those dearest to me, to induce you to swerve from the course which truth and honour distinctly point out. Whatever may seem to be the consequences, we are both bound to follow this, and we have but to feel that, if need be, we are ready to make great sacrifices to receive the requisite faith and strength. Believe me," she concluded, and her voice trembled slightly, "whatever happens, I shall feel that you have given me proofs of a friendship upon which I may depend."

I pressed the hand I still held, and I felt the touch was sacred. "Ah," thought I, as I left the room, and was conscious that the gentle influence of her I had parted from was still resting upon me, "that is the right kind of spirit-medium. There is a magnetism in that slender finger which supports and purifies." O my hardened and material readers! don't suppose that because I know you will laugh at the idea of a purifying or invigorating magnetism I shall hesitate to write exactly what I feel on such matters. If I refrain from saying a great deal more, it is not because I shrink from your ridicule but from your ignorance. You may not believe that the pearls exist; I honestly admit that they are not yet in my possession, but I have seen those who own them, and, unfortunately, also I have seen the animals before whom they have been cast. And you, my dear young ladies, do not ignore the responsibility which the influence you are able to exercise over young men imposes upon you. You need not call it magnetism unless you like, but be sure that there is that conveyed in a touch or a glance which elevates or degrades him upon whom it is bestowed, according as you preserve the purity and simplicity of your inmost natures. If you would only regard yourselves in the light of female missionaries to that benighted tribe of lavender-gloved young gentlemen who flutter about you like moths round a candle, you would send them away glowing and happy, instead of singeing their wings. If, when these butterflies come to sip, you would give them honey instead of poison, they would not forsake you as they do now for the gaudy flowers which are too near you. I know what you have to contend against—the scheming mothers who bring you up to the "Daughticultural Show," labelled and decorated, and put up to competition as likely prize-winners—who deliberately expose you to the first rush of your first seasons, and mercilessly watch you as you are swept along by the tearing stream—who see you without compunction cast away on sandbanks of worldliness, where you remain till you become as "hard" and as "fast" as those you find stranded there before you. Here your minds become properly, or rather improperly, opened. You hear, for the first time, to your astonishment, young men talked of by their Christian or nick names—their domestic life canvassed, their eligibility discussed, and the varied personal experiences through which your "hard and fast" friends have passed, related.

Then, better prepared for the rest of the voyage, you start again, and venture a little on your own account. What bold swimmers you are becoming now! How you laugh and defy the rocks and reefs upon which you are ultimately destined to split! Already you look back with surprise to the time when almost everything you heard shocked you. What an immense amount of unnecessary knowledge you have acquired since then, and how recklessly you display it! Do you think it has softened and elevated you? Do you think the moral contact which should be life-giving to those who know you, benefits them?

It is not true, because young men behave heartlessly, that you must flirt "in self-defence," as you call it. When a warfare of this kind once begins, it is difficult to fix the responsibility; but if one side left off, the occupation of the other would be gone. If you want to revenge yourselves on these fickle youths—*strike!* as they do in the manufacturing districts. Conceive the wholesome panic you would cause, if you combined into "unions" like the working-classes, and every girl in London bound herself not to flirt for the entire season!

Unless you do something of this kind soon, you will reverse the whole system of nature. The men will be the candles and you the moths; they will be the flowers, and you the butterflies. If all the brothers in London persist in trying to imitate their sisters, and all the sisters ape their brothers, what a nice confusion we shall arrive at! The reason I preach to you and not to them now, is, because I think I have a better chance with the mind of a masculine young woman than with that of a feminine young man. If you only knew what a comfort it would be to talk sense instead of that incessant chaff, you would read a little more. I don't object to your riding in the Park—the abominable constitution of society makes it almost the only opportunity of seeing and talking to those you like without being talked about; but you need not rush off for a drive in the carriage immediately after lunch, just because you are too restless to stay at home.

First, the Park and young men, then lunch, then Marshall and Snelgrove, then tea and young men again, then dinner, drums, and balls, and young men till three A.M. That is the tread-wheel you have chosen to turn without the smallest profit to yourself or any one else. If I seem to speak strongly, it is because my heart yearns over you. I belonged once to the lavender-gloved tribe myself, and though I have long since abandoned the hunting-grounds of my youth, I would give the world to see them happy and innocent. Moreover, I know you too well to imagine that I have written a word which will offend you. Far from it. We shall be warmer and closer friends ever after; but I am strongly afraid mamma will disapprove. She will call 'Piccadilly' "highly improper," and say that it is a book she has not allowed any of "her girls" to read. I don't want to preach disobedience; but there are modes well known to my fair young friends of reading books which mamma forbids, and I trust that they will never read one against her wish which may leave a more injurious impression upon their minds than 'Piccadilly.'

PART V.

THE FLESH.

PICCADILLY, *June*.

Somebody ought to compile a handbook for *débutants* and *débutantes*, setting forth the most approved modes of procuring invitations to balls and parties during the London season. Not only would it be a very invaluable guide now, but it would be interesting for posterity to refer to as illustrating the manners and customs of their ancestors, and accounting for the hereditary taint of snobbism which is probably destined to characterise in an eminent degree the population of the British Isles. "En Angleterre," said a cynical Dutch diplomatist, "numéro deux va chez numéro un, pour s'en glorifier auprès de numéro trois." Had he gone to the Bodwinkle ball, he would have remarked a curious inversion of his aphorism, for there it was *numéro un* who went down to *numéro deux*. But I must leave it to Van den Bosch (that, I think, was his name) to discover what there was to boast about to number three. He was evidently a profound philosopher, but I doubt his getting to the bottom of this great social problem. To do so he would have to look at it free from all petty prejudice, recognising its sublime as well as its ridiculous features. Why did Duchesses struggle to be asked to Bodwinkle's? I almost think a new phase of snobbism is cropping out, and the rivalry will be to try, not who can rise highest, but who can sink lowest, in the social scale. The fashionable world is so *blasé* of itself that it has positively become tired of worshipping wealth, unless its owners possess the charm of extreme vulgarity. Its taste has become so vitiated by being unnaturally excited and pandered to, that we shall have to invent some new object of ambition. Why, for instance, should not a select clique of Oxford Street shopkeepers give a series of parties which might become the rage for one season? They have only to get two or three leaders of *ton* to patronise them at first, and be very exclusive and select in their invitations afterwards, to insure success. A year or two ago the thing to do was Cremorne; why not have an Oxford Street year? The

Bodwinkle tendency will result at last in its being the great ambition of a man's life to get his daughters asked to "a little music and a few friends" at his bootmaker's.

In Paris, which is becoming rapidly impregnated with this spirit, that city being in a very receptive condition for everything bad from all parts of the world—in Paris, I say, they have made a very good start, as any of my fair friends who have patronised Mr Worth's afternoon tea-parties in the Rue de la Paix will readily acknowledge. They will bear testimony to the good taste of the milliner, and I to the bad taste of his customers. That vain women in the highest circles of Parisian fashion can, in an eager rivalry to display as much of their backs as possible, endeavour to obtain the especial patronage of a man-dressmaker, by accepting his invitations to tea, should be a warning to you, O gentle English dames! of what you may come to. Why sacrifice self-respect and propriety to shoulder-straps? Why insist upon it that there is only one man in the world who knows how to cut out a dress behind? Supposing he can bring it an inch lower down than anybody else—if you give that inch, beware of the ell. Why, oh why, advertise your clothes in the newspapers? Is it not enough to puff your dinner-parties in the public journals at so much a "notice," without paying 15s. apiece to your dressmaker to put your names into the 'Morning Post,' coupled with your wearing apparel, every time you go to Court? If you persist in the practice, let me recommend you, as a measure of economy, to put in your own advertisements. The press charge is 10s. 6d.; the dressmaker pockets the other 4s. 6d. Or else be generous: why keep the whole advertisement to yourself? let the poor dressmaker put her name in as having furnished the raiment, and she will, perhaps, let you off the 4s. 6d.; otherwise, you may do it still cheaper by bills on hoardings—

IMMENSE ATTRACTION!

The Marchioness of Scilly will appear at Court on the —— inst. Train glacé—poult de soie bouillionée, &c.

I am not sure that to attend the professional social gatherings of a Parisian "undressmaker" and pay him twenty francs a "look" is not less objectionable, but this is the British way of worshipping the same idol. This vein of reflection was suggested to me by Bodwinkle's ball. Talk of sermons in stones! they are nothing to the sermons contained in drums and balls.

First, I have already let my readers into the secret history of that ball. I have told them how Lady Broadhem and Spiffy Goldtip combined their resources and launched the Bodwinkles in Vanity Fair with a gorgeous mansion and Lady Mundane's invitation list. To describe all Spiffy's exertions in the Bodwinkle cause for some days prior to the ball would be impossible. To tell of the extraordinary suggestions that Bodwinkle was continually making with reference to the decoration of the banisters, the arrangements for supper, and the utter ignorance he displayed throughout of the nature of the enterprise upon which he had embarked, would occupy more space than I can afford. To give a list of the guests would be superfluous, as they were very accurately reported in the columns of the 'Morning Post.' In spite of all Spiffy could do, Bodwinkle would insist upon inviting a number of his own friends, and nearly ruined the party irretrievably by allowing one man to bring his daughters. However, as Mrs B. did not take the slightest notice of them, and as they knew nobody, they went away early. Nevertheless, as Lady Veriphast said, "There were all kinds of people that one had never seen in one's life before." This was the great mistake. People don't yet humiliate themselves to get invitations to meet people they never saw before. They may come to that, but at present nothing is worth going to unless all society wants to go: then anything is. Now Spiffy had so managed, that by a judicious system of puffing he had excited immense interest in the Bodwinkle ball—he had been morally bill-sticking it in all the clubs for weeks past. He had told the most *répandu* young dancing men that it would be impossible for him to get them invitations. If Bodwinkle had been General Tom Thumb, and Spiffy had been Barnum, he could not have achieved a greater success. He had insisted upon Bodwinkle having Mrs B. painted by the most fashionable artist and exhibited in the Academy, where the hanging committee, some of whom were at the ball afterwards, gave it a good place, and the

'Times' critic gave it half a column. Until then he had kept her dark. No one had ever seen Mrs Bodwinkle, except three or four literary men, who discreetly and mysteriously alluded to her intellect, and a naughty duke, who indiscreetly and less mysteriously alluded to her charms. People began to want to make Mrs Bodwinkle's acquaintance some time before the ball, but she resolutely denied herself. The only men who were let into the secret were Bower, Scraper, and a few others skilled in the art of socially advertising. Their principal function consisted in asking every one of their friends for some time before whether they were going to the Bodwinkle ball. It oozed out, through Spiffy, that I knew something of Bodwinkle, and the result was that I was bombarded with requests to procure invitations. This was the style of note that arrived incessantly. This is from Mary, Marchioness of Pimlico:—

"DEAR LORD FRANK,—Lady Mundane tells me that you are one of the privileged few who can get invitations to the Bodwinkles'. Please exert your interest in my favour. You know this is Alice's first season.—Yours truly,

"MARY PIMLICO."

Here is another one:—

"DEAR LORD FRANK,—Do *please* get an invitation for *my very great friend*, Amy Rumsort, for the Bodwinkles'. She is most anxious to go, *for very particular* reasons. I will tell you them when we meet. Spiffy Goldtip sent mamma mine, but declines to come to the front about Amy.—Yours most sincerely, HARRIET WYLDE."

"Wild Harrie" is the name by which this young lady is usually known among her sporting friends. She is a promising *débutante*, and very properly calls herself "first favourite" of the season.

"Dear me," thought I, as I opened a series of similar epistles, "if I were the head of a public department, who only recommended honours to be given to those who applied for them oftenest, and if all these were meritorious public servants wanting C.B.'s, or gallant soldiers anxious for Victoria Crosses, they could not beg more pertinaciously and unblushingly." And I made a list of the petitioners, leaving out those who had written to me without knowing me, and went to the club, where I intrusted them to Spiffy, with a peremptory request that he would distribute the required invitations upon pain of my financial displeasure.

Spiffy gave me some curious statistics about invitations and the means employed to obtain them. Three ladies who never asked him to their parties, and whom he had therefore left out, though all more or less leaders of the *beau monde*, actually wrote to Mrs Bodwinkle in various strains—one was a threatening, the other an appealing letter, and the third assumed that she had been omitted by mistake. Two young gentlemen had the impertinence, after trying every other mode in vain, actually to call on Mrs Bodwinkle, and extract invitations from that bewildered woman, who was too much frightened to refuse them. Bodwinkle was not idle in the House, and two Liberals and an extreme Radical, all young, unable to resist temptation, voted against the Government on the promise of invitations. As for Spiffy, even he was acquiring fresh social experience, and tells me he can scarcely resist entering upon a pecuniary *exploitation* of his position in society. "There is," said that enterprising and original individual, "so much to be done by a man of genius. Just look what is open to me in this line,——

"'Families in the country anxious that their sons should be well *lancés* in the society of the metropolis, are requested to apply to the Honourable Spiffington Goldtip. Invitations to the most fashionable parties obtained at a reasonable amount. Charges moderate for introductions to Clubs. No charge whatever for introductions to noblemen.'

"Or in this line,—

"'To Debutantes and Others in want of Chaperonage.— Young ladies whose mothers are invalids, or are from some cause considered objectionable by society, or who have only step-mothers, or who are orphans with unkind or Evangelical relations, or who are unexpectedly at the last moment deprived of their natural protectors, on applying to the undersigned will be provided with suitable chaperons. The undersigned begs to notify that his stock of chaperons will bear the strictest examination as to character, and have all at one time or other moved in the highest circles of society. No debutante or young lady whose birth and antecedents do not entitle her to the same privilege need apply. SPIFFINGTON GOLDTIP.'

"Then the *pendant* to this would be,—

"'To Married Women or Widows without Daughters.— Married women, or widows without daughters, who have either dropped out of society or are in danger of dropping out, in consequence of there being no special reason why they should be kept in, and who are capable of undertaking the duties of chaperon, are requested to apply to the Honourable Spiffington Goldtip. The Hon. S. G. has a large stock of debutantes, and other young ladies in want of chaperons, always on hand. The strictest references given and required.'

"You may laugh," Spiffy went on, "but I assure you the sort of successes I have in my own line are quite astonishing. Look what a hit I've made with Wild Harrie—her mother, Lady Wylde, you remember, was her husband's brother's governess. Well, I said plainly to her, 'You will ruin that girl's chances if you attempt to force her on society in your own way. You can't afford to entertain upon the right scale, and you won't be asked anywhere unless you do, for there is a set going to be made against Harriet. If you will leave her to me, I know her strong points, and will see her through the whole business as if she was my own sister.'" I must here remark *en passant* that Spiffy is apparently capable of doing the most unselfish things, and of taking an infinity of trouble upon himself out of pure good-nature.

"What was your *modus operandi*?" I asked.

"Oh, it was all plain sailing enough. The first thing to provide was a popular chaperon, and the second a special reputation. Now Harrie is a wonderful rider, and knows a horse thoroughly. Then she looks like a high-bred Arab herself, though her mother was a governess, and I felt sure Dick Helter would fall a victim. So I introduced her to the Helters. As Lady Jane goes in for safeness, she does not like married women, and always smiles most kindly upon any girl that pleases her husband; so I knew if I could get Harrie by her side on the top of Helter's drag, the next step was a certainty, and that I had secured my chaperon. The result has fully justified my expectations. Harrie has secured the box-seat *en permanence*, went down to the Derby on Helter's drag, and won a pot on the French horse under his judicious advice. Little Haultort, and all the other men who lost to her, adore her of course, and all the girls in London hate her; but whenever the mammas object to asking her on account of 'that horrid Lady Wylde,' I floor all opposition by saying, 'Oh, Lady Jane Helter will bring her.' I wonder," said Spiffy, with a sigh, "when she has made her little game, whether she will remember to whom she owed it?"

"Now, do you find much ingratitude of this kind?" I asked, inquiringly.

"No," said Spiffy. "I must say on the whole my experience of the world in this respect is, that it is not so black as it is painted. It is true that I attribute its gratitude chiefly to laziness. For instance, in my own case, so long as I hold the position I do in society, people who insisted upon being ungrateful to me would find it hard work. By the way, I observe you don't go out as much as you used—how's that?" This was no business of Spiff's, so I said sublimely, "Because the aristocracy bore me, and the middle classes grate upon my nerves.—But about this little girl: she is rather an ally of mine, so you must see that her friend, Miss Rumsort, has the card."

"It is too bad!" broke out Spiffy. "The way that girl and her married sister are trying to take the world by storm is intolerable. It does not matter whether they know the people they apply to or not, it is always the same story. She pretends she is tremendously in love with Larkington because he goes everywhere, and her sister looks sentimental, and tries to work upon your feelings about 'poor Amy,' whose only object in life is to meet him; but it is all a dodge to get asked. She cares no more for Larkington than for me. Now, I'll be bound Wild Harrie put something about *very particular reasons* in her note to you."

"Well," said I, astonished at Spiffy's penetration, and at the new views of life he was placing before me, "I must admit that that phrase did occur."

"Of course it did; why, it is one of the regular forms of 'extorting invitations under false pretences.' I want the police to interfere, but it seems, although they are doubtless begging-letters, containing fraudulent misrepresentations, there is some difficulty about bringing them within the terms of the Act."

"Never mind—live and let live—send her the invitation. It seems to me, my dear Spiffy, that you and the Bodwinkles and Miss Rumsort are all in the same line of life, so you should not be too hard upon her. As a matter of policy, social adventurers should do what they can for each other."

Spiffy's face flushed, for if he had lost the conscience, he still retained the consciousness, of a gentleman, and he felt the reproach.

Just at this moment, Mr Wog, who had been elected an honorary member of the "Piccadilly," and was standing, unconsciously to us, listening to our conversation, struck in, and averted the retort which was rising to Spiffy's lips.

"I guess," he said, turning to Spiffy, for whose talents he evidently entertained a high admiration, "that I could give you a few hints, from my own experiences in New York, that might help you in your line of business. My own, sir, in that city, was quite similar to yours in this. You operate at night in Mayfair, and by day 'On 'Change.' Well, sir, I had two spheres of operation, one was on Wall Street, and the other on Fifth Avenue. In fact, I may say that Wall Street is the broad and flowery road that leads to Fifth Avenue. The trouble with operators in this country is, they don't understand how to do things on a large scale. Now the first thing I did when I went to do business in New York, was to keep a judge."

"To keep a judge?" said Spiffy with amazement.

"Why, yes. How can you operate freely if you are afraid of the law? Besides his regular monthly allowance, my judge gets a percentage on every one of my financial enterprises which are fraudulent according to the letter of the statute. Then it costs me a good deal to manage to get all my lawsuits tried in his court. Besides, I have to keep a number of members of both the Houses of the Legislature at Albany regularly retained, and to put a big pile on one side for lobby operations at Washington, to say nothing about keeping the pockets of police and custom-house officers and other small fry well lined. The press alone swallows up the fifth of all I make. How do you suppose I could ever have accomplished my celebrated combination by which I got four large railroads under my control, and sold a secret issue of twenty millions of stock for fifteen millions, without ever paying one dime of it to any of the companies, if I had not stopped the mouths of the lawyers, politicians, and newspapers with greenbacks? Why, sir, I have ruined more whole families in one day by one of my financial operations, than any other man in the United States has in a month; and by the extraordinary novelty, grandeur, variety, and success of my undertakings, I have won the admiration, envy, and respect of the majority of my countrymen."

Spiffy seemed deeply impressed by the superior force and originality of conception displayed by Mr Wog—no indication of these qualities appearing on his calm exterior. "Of what nature are your operations in Fifth Avenue?" he asked.

"Oh, purely social," Mr Wog replied. "You see the aristocracy of New York require to be approached in a very special way. You can enter into the ranks of the upper ten, either by becoming a pillar of a fashionable church, or by driving the fastest trotters and handsomest four-in-hand teams in Central Park, or by the help of Mr Pink."

"By the help of Mr Pink?" said I, interrogatively.

"Yes. He corresponds to our friend Spiffy here. He is the sexton of St Grace's, the most fashionable church in New York; and when you have made your pile, and want to start in fashionable life, and don't know who to invite, he makes out your list, and puts the invitations to your first ball in the prayer-books of the congregation. It imparts a sort of odour of sanctity to our entertainments, which is exceedingly gratifying to our most refined circles."

"I suppose," said I, "now that your social and financial position are secured, you will run for Congress."

"Sir," said Mr Wog, sternly, "when I explained to you the nature of my commercial success, it was to convey to you the idea of my smartness, not of my meanness. I am not aware of having said anything to lead you to suppose that I could so far degrade myself as to become a politician."

"What a comfort it will be," I remarked, "when the rotten old despotisms of Europe, and the political ambitions that belong to them, shall have crumbled to the dust, and when we have instead the free and glorious institutions of the West, which seem to offer nothing to tempt a man from the ennobling pursuit of hard cash!" But Mr Wog failed to appreciate the force of my remark, as he was intently endeavouring to catch the purport of a very private conversation carried on by a group a few yards off, towards which he gradually edged, in the hope that he might be able either to acquire or impart some interesting information.

Spiffy looked more humbled and crestfallen than I had ever seen him; but remembering that he had still a score unsettled, in consequence of the remark which Mr Wog's arrival had interrupted, he said, maliciously,—

"By the way, what is the real state of the case about you and Lady Ursula? I don't apologise for asking, as I am sure you must want the right version to be known both for your sake and hers."

"The right version is simply that I neither am at this moment nor ever have been engaged to Lady Ursula."

"Then why did you tell Helter you were, and why are you pulling the family through their difficulties?"

"Because Helter was provoking me almost as much as you are, though I admit that is no reason why I should not have told the truth. As for the motives which actuate me in meddling in those pecuniary transactions in which you and Lady Broadhem are implicated, I am afraid you would not understand them if I were to attempt to explain them. It is a complicated business altogether. We shall get through it most satisfactorily by each minding our own share of it," I said significantly, and I walked off to a table where Broadhem was writing letters. I had not seen him since my interview with his sister. He looked gloomy and discontented, and gave me a cold glance of recognition. "How are you, Broadhem? I suppose Lady Ursula told you the result of our conversation," I said in a low tone, and took a chair by his side.

He nodded sulkily, and showed a disposition to cut me. My last few words with Spiffy had not left me in a mood to be cut unresistingly, so I said sharply, "Well, I hope both you and Lady Broadhem will contradict the perfectly unfounded report you were the means of spreading. I need not say that I shall do my share, and I trust that you will profit by the lesson you have received not to interfere in matters of this sort again."

"I tell you what it is, Frank," said Broadhem, who felt that somehow I was more to blame than he was, but who was taken aback by my turning the tables upon him so suddenly; "if it was not that duelling is exploded, and that it would be against my principles at any rate, I would shoot you."

"By way of helping to clear your property of its encumbrances," I added. "Your mother has put everything into my hands, and I can do pretty much what I please with the whole family."

"Can you?" said Broadhem, with a grim smile. "The only thing that consoles me in the whole affair is, that you will find that you have got a little score to settle with my mother. If you knew her as well as I do, you would not anticipate the interview with pleasure. As for Ursula, I suppose she knows her own business best, but I don't envy her the life she is likely to lead either."

"The alarming interview you threaten me with gives me no uneasiness," I said, "but perhaps it may be as well that you should let Lady Broadhem know that the fact of my not being engaged to her daughter will not interfere with the arrangements I am making to put the money matters of the family right."

"Why! you can't mean that!" said Broadhem, thunderstruck at this unexpected announcement; and he looked at me with a glance of affectionate interest. "You must be mad."

"Did your sister tell you so?" I asked.

"Once she did make a mysterious speech, and I really think she meant to imply something of the sort. However, of course, I am only joking. I need not say I hope, under the circumstances, it will be long before you recover your sanity."

"Are you going to the Bodwinkles' to-morrow?" said I, doing a little of Bower and Scraper's work.

"Good gracious, no! I am bored to death with having to answer the question. The trouble my mother has taken to get those people invitations is something amazing. She even wanted me to go, though she does not approve of balls, and never let me learn to dance."

"Let me introduce you to Miss Geary. You are not too old to begin."

"No," said Broadhem; "I have started on the other tack, and people would say it was inconsistent; besides, none of the young thinking men of the day dance, even though they may not be religious. I don't suppose that there is a single man in the Century dances."

This observation struck me as so preposterous that I could only account for it by supposing that, for the first time in his life, Broadhem had condescended to "chaff."

"Not 'a man' in the ideal sense, I daresay; but the boys are not more backward in this century than in any former one."

"Boys!" said Broadhem, indignantly; "there are no boys in the 'Century;' the 'Century' is a club that meets twice a-week. I don't go on Sunday nights myself; but some Thursday night I will take you," and Broadhem plunged back into the correspondence in which I had interrupted him, while I strolled home down Piccadilly moralising on—the Century.

I don't frequent balls now, but I went to Bodwinkle's for a variety of reasons. One was, that I knew I should see everybody, and have an opportunity of informing the public correctly about my own affairs. Another, that I should be able to talk over some business matters with Bodwinkle, at a moment when he might possibly be more pliant than I usually found him in the City.

Every soul was at Bodwinkle's—coroneted carriages filled the square; a crowd of draggled men and women formed a line six or eight deep on each side of the awning, and between them fine ladies hurried across the pavement, encouraged and complimented by familiar linkmen, and very particular that the 'Morning Post' reporter, seated at a table in the hall, should take down their names accurately. The stairs were so crowded that Bodwinkle, who looked like one of his own footmen, and stood at the top of them, facing his wife, was red and apoplectic from pressure. His "lady," as I heard one of his City friends call her, had achieved the greatest object of her ambition in this life, which consisted in grinning vacantly, and curtsying perpetually to people she had never seen in her life before, and every one of whom despised her for entertaining them.

"Curious idea of the climax of earthly enjoyment," I remarked to Lady Veriphast, who was so tightly wedged between the banisters and a rather highly-scented ambassador from Central Asia, that she spoke with difficulty; "I suppose it must be a pleasure to be at the top of one's own ladder, like our hostess there, when so many are trying to climb it."

"Do *not* philosophise in that ridiculous way; don't you see I am suffering agonies?" said Lady Veriphast, in a tone of suppressed anguish. "Pinch this horrid barbarian in front of me or I shall faint."

"Madam," I overheard a well-known voice say in a nasal tone close to me, "allow me to remark, that for a hand, arm, and wrist, I have not seen anything since I have been in England like that owned by your daughter Mary;" and Mr Wog complacently edged himself from the side of Lady Mundane to that of the daughter he had eulogised, and who audibly asked Scraper to get between her and that horrid man.

"Just what one deserves for coming to such a place," said Lady Mundane furiously, who, by the way, had repeatedly asked Wog to her own parties.

"I have often remarked, sir," said Mr Wog, who I think overheard this observation, turning to me, "that the ladies in your country allow quite a singular effect to be produced in their hair. If you will cast your eye down the stair you will observe a young person on the landing, the parting of whose hair, for the space of one inch on either side, is black, while the two large bunches on her temples are red. That, sir, is a phenomenon I have not remarked in my own country."

"Don't you know how it happens?" said that spiteful old Lady Catchpole, whose eyes twinkled with malice as she explained to Mr Wog that, when the hair had been thoroughly dyed it could only recover its natural colour by this slow process, but that usually the effect was concealed by a *postiche*; and she looked hard at Lady Veriphast, whose hair was suspiciously *crepé*, and who wished it to be supposed that she blushed because she was still under the pressure of the Asiatic ambassador.

"What is the exact meaning of the term *postiche*?" asked Mr Wog, who observed Lady Veriphast's confusion, and whose thirst for information seemed to increase with his powers of making himself disagreeable; "I guess it must mean some kind of wig."

"No," said Lady Catchpole; "anything false which is well made up we call a *postiche*; it need not be exactly a wig."

"Nor yet a Tory," interrupted Wog, with more readiness than I gave him credit for. "I calculate you should call a Liberal Conservative a *postiche*. It seems to me the most popular political platform in this country at your next elections is going to be *postiche*."

"Look, my dear," said Lady Pimlico to Lady Mundane, "there are the two Frenchwomen," and she directed universal attention to the last importations from the Continent, Madame la Princesse de Biaisée à la Queue, and La Baronne de Colté, whose fame had preceded them from Paris, and who created such a sensation that the general hum on the stairs increased, and the whole society collected there audibly criticised the new-comers. "Why, positively the tall one has got her hair done *en papillon*—I thought it had gone out—I suppose her face won't bear being *coiffé à la grècque*; and the other is outrageously painted." This remark was made so loud that both ladies looked up, but failed to check the running fire of comments which their dress and appearance suggested.

"They say the Princess makes up for her want of looks by her legs," drawled out Larkington to Lady Veriphast; "but I am afraid we shall not have an opportunity of seeing them to-night, it is so crowded."

"They are not worth looking at; I saw them at a fancy ball in Paris," said Lady Veriphast, "and I assure you you would be disappointed. By the way, have you the least notion who the Bodwinkles are?"

"Not I," replied Larkington. "I did not come here to make their acquaintance, nor I hope did you."

I think Mrs Bodwinkle heard the speech—for it is customary in good society to make remarks about one's neighbours in rather a loud tone—as she coloured a little when she was pointed out to Larkington by the fat butler as the person to whom he was expected to bow. Poor woman! she probably thought he would be embarrassed when he found out his proximity; but Larkington is above any such weakness, and sauntered on after Lady Veriphast, with whom he has *affichéd* himself for the last few weeks, to the great comfort of Veriphast, who has long been desirous of making his wife share the scandal which has attached to his name for some time past.

"And it is for this, my dear Mrs Bodwinkle," I thought, "that you have given up your villa at Clapham, and the friends that respectfully worshipped at the Bodwinkle shrine, who gazed upon you with reverend upturned eyes, instead of irreverent upturned noses, like the present company! Do you think, when you have blazed for a moment and gone out like a blue-light, that you will know how to find your way in the dark back to Clapham, or that you will be able to collect your old congregation? Will not new Bodwinkles have arisen above the suburban horizon, or will the departed glories of your rapid but bright passage across the firmament of fashion always secure you an audience who will gladly listen to your wonderful experiences in the great world, to whom you will recount the devotion manifested towards you by certain noblemen, and the slights you received at the hands of certain noblewomen, and who will stare when you describe the Broadhem-Spiffy combination which sent you up like a rocket, and the sudden collapse of that combination which will assuredly bring you down like a stick? Never mind, Mrs B.; whatever happens, nothing short of a fire can deprive you of the basket of fashionable cards which will be left upon you during the season, and which, carefully treasured with your dinner *menus*, will be a lasting evidence of the reality of that social triumph which might otherwise seem like the 'baseless fabric of a dream.'"

And this consideration reminds me that I possess middle-class readers, who may positively doubt the truth of the picture which I am endeavouring to give them of the society in which Mrs Bodwinkle now found herself. They will not have the advantage of hearing from the lips of that good lady these wonderful traits of the manners and customs of this, to them, mysterious class. And therefore they will fail to see any particular merit in what they may suppose to be merely a flippant delineation of a purely ideal state of society. My dear readers, I should be no more competent to invent a state of society so eccentric in its habits and constitution as this of London cream, than I should be to write an account of lion-hunting like the late lamented Jules Gerard. That was a real strain upon the imaginative and constructive faculties; I aspire to no such talent, but simply contemplate hyperbolically a certain phase of contemporary civilisation. If, by way of a little pastime, I put Mayfair into a fancy dress, it only appears in its true colours and becomes fancy-fair, with a great deal of show and very little substance; so I dress it up as it pleases me, but I invent nothing. I confine myself strictly to the stage properties. You in the pit or gallery may be too far off to see, but I assure you I have avoided anything beyond the exaggeration permissible in a caricature. As I know your imitative faculties, dear middle classes, I can conscientiously assure you that you may take 'Piccadilly' as a guide upon which to frame your own society. Take the most successful costermonger of the neighbourhood and erect him into a Bodwinkle, and fall down upon your knees before the most opulent pawnbroker of your parish; and you will feel that you are only performing, on a humble scale, the same act of worship as those above you.

Lady Jane Helter, followed by Wild Harrie, came up while I was thus musing. "So, Lord Frank," she said, "you are not to be congratulated after all? I suppose you heard of our dinner at the Whitechapels'? We all thought your conduct very incomprehensible. I assure you Lady Broadhem seemed as much in the dark as the rest of us."

"And you want to be enlightened?" said I. "Well, it has been a social *canard* throughout, which I did not at first think worth contradicting. There must be a certain number every season."

"I am sure we want them more than ever now," said Wild Harrie. "Was there ever such an utterly flat season? I only went to two balls last week, and, as they say at 'the corner,' 'there was positively nothing doing.'"

"It is not the same in every corner," said I; "look opposite," and I pointed out Larkington and Lady Veriphast snugly ensconced in a recess.

"Poor Amy! I am afraid that won't suit her book," said Wild Harrie. "She is really devoted to Lord Larkington. I told her to hedge, but she says she has too much heart. By the way, I want to have a little private conversation with you. Take me to have a cup of tea, or a quadrille, or something"—this in rather a low tone, not for Lady Jane's benefit; and we sidled off through the throng, leaving Lady Jane at the doorway, which, in the absence of her ladyship, does duty as chaperon.

"Do you know, Lord Frank," said my companion, "that it really was very kind of you to get me the invitation you did, and that I can appreciate kindness; can you guess how?"

"By asking me to do something else for you," I said.

"Exactly," she said, laughing; "but this time it will not perhaps be quite so easy. I want you to get me a card for Lady Broadhem's on Thursday week."

"For Lady Broadhem's!" said I, astounded. "How on earth did you come to hear of it? Why, it is a meeting, not a party. A few Christian friends are going to hear the Bishop of the Caribbee Islands describe the state of mission-work in his diocese. You would be bored to death."

"Indeed I should not," said Wild Harrie. "I have a brother in India; and I have heard so much about the heathen. Besides, I want to make Lady Ursula's acquaintance."

"I really don't think," said I, a good deal puzzled, "that you will find it a very congenial atmosphere, but I am sure nobody can know Lady Ursula without deriving benefit, so I should feel too glad to be the means of making you acquainted; but Lady Jane will never take you."

"Oh, mamma will; you know her brother was a clergyman. Promise. Don't forget—one for me and one for mamma. Now I must leave you; I quite forgot I was engaged to little Haultort for this dance, and there he is hunting for me everywhere," and she dragged me to the spot where that young gentleman was stroking a fluffy mustache, with an imbecile air.

"Do you call that hunting?" said I; "He must be in chase of ideas."

"Of course he is. Now watch him catch big *idée fixe*," and she placed herself before him. Poor youth! how he coloured and stammered, as a ray of intelligence illumined his countenance! "So that is the way you keep your engagements, Lord Haultort, is it? Well, you have forfeited your dance"—the ray went out—"but you may take me back to Lady Jane." The ray came back again; he was sufficiently experienced to know what that meant, and Lord Haultort disappeared into the next room with his *idée fixe* on his arm, and I looked the other way half an hour after, when I passed the corresponding recess in which Larkington and Lady Veriphast were still sitting, and saw who were there.

"I wonder what that little girl wants to know the Broadhems for?" I ruminated, and for some time I was positively fool enough to continue to wonder.

"I tell you what it is, Goldtip," I overheard Bodwinkle say, "that idea of yours about giving presents is all humbug; we've got the people here, what do you want to give them presents for?"

"In the first place," retorted Spiffy, "they will never come again unless you keep faith with them now, for I have been giving it out specially that no expense was to be spared; and in the second place, as you have got all the presents made up in ribbons, &c., what else are you to do with them? The girls will be terribly disappointed."

Bodwinkle shook his head sulkily, and Spiffy, seeing me, adroitly turned the conversation. "I was talking over the prospects of the approaching election, Frank, with Bodwinkle, and telling him how much you could assist us with your influence in Shuffleborough; it seems to me that he is likely to be turned out unless your brother-in-law, Sir John Stepton, will come to the rescue. It would be well worth your while, Bodwinkle, to let Lady Broadhem's matter stand over until you have made sure of your seat," said Spiffy, looking significantly at me.

"Oh, certainly," said Bodwinkle, "if you will secure your brother-in-law's adhesion to our plans. You will find me very amenable in that unfortunate affair of Lady Broadhem's. I know what an interest you take in it, and I am sure, for your sake, if not for hers—ahem," and Bodwinkle, quite unconscious that he was behaving like a scoundrel, smiled upon me blandly.

"It seems to me," said I, "that, considering what you owe to Lady Broadhem," and I looked round the crowded room, "you ought not to be too hard upon her."

"Ah, well, I must admit that her ladyship and our friend Goldtip here are doing their best to balance the account; but I have made it a principle through life never to be satisfied with anything short of my full money's worth; and I don't even feel now, if you make my election a certainty, that we shall be more than square."

"What are your other principles besides that of getting your full money's worth?" said I, with a sneer, that was lost upon Bodwinkle.

"High Tory," he replied, promptly. "None of your Liberal Conservatives for me this time—that did well enough last election."

"But Stepton is an absolute Radical," said I.

"Exactly: that is why he is so important. You see the fact is—here, Goldtip, explain our little game; it is all his idea, and he can put it better than me."

I knew from the bold defiant way in which Spiffy raised his eyes to mine that his original and unscrupulous genius had conceived a *coup d'état* of some kind, so I listened curiously.

"I am going to stand for Shuffleborough, and it is I who want Sir John Stepton's vote and influence," he announced, calmly.

"You!" said I, amazed; "what are you going to stand as? and who is going to pay your expenses?"

"I am going to stand as an extreme Liberal, and Bodwinkle as a regular old Tory. He is going to pay my expenses. We are going to strike out an entirely new line, and have convictions. He can't come the Liberal Conservative this time, as one of the Liberals who is very popular has gone in rather extensively for the Moderate Conservatives. So there is nothing for it but to come forward as an out-and-out Tory, and put me up as a Radical; by these means we hope to floor both the fellows that are trying the trimming game. Of course I am not intended to come in—I only split the party."

"But if you stand, one of the others will retire. Look at what has just happened at Westminster."

"Then Bodwinkle starts his wife's cousin Tom—why, he is rich enough to keep all three Liberals in the field to fight him if necessary; and you are pluck to the backbone, aint you, old fellow?" and Spiffy slapped Bodwinkle on the back.

"Perhaps you would like to see our addresses," he went on,—"here they are; I wrote them both. I shall issue mine first, and Bodwinkle's a day or two after."

"May I take them home to read?" I asked.

"Oh, certainly, and frame your own on their model if you like," said Spiffy, laughing; "they'll be the neatest thing out in addresses, I assure you."

"Mr Goldtip, I wish you would exert yourself, instead of talking politics with Mr B.," said Mrs Bodwinkle, coming up; "there are all sorts of things to arrange, and I am sure I don't know who is to take who down to supper;" and Spiffy was carried away upon special service.

"Good-night, Bodwinkle," said I; "your ball is a great success, but I am an early man, and hot rooms don't suit me. I understand the political situation thoroughly now, and without pledging myself to anything, will see what is to be done."

"Of course, all in the most perfect confidence; it would never do for Stepton to suspect what we were at."

"Oh, it would be absolute ruin. There is just one question I should like to ask, Can you give me your solemn word that in all this you have no other motive but the single one of being of use to your country?"

"Eh!" said Bodwinkle, with his eyes rather wide open.

"I repeat," said I, slowly, "Is your only object in getting into Parliament that you may be of use to the country? or is it that the country may be of use to you?"

"I must ask you one in return," said Bodwinkle: "Will it depend upon my answer whether or not you exert yourself in my favour?"

"Entirely," said I.

"Then, my dear Lord Frank," said Bodwinkle, affectionately grasping my hand, "believe me, that so far as I am concerned, and I can say the same for Goldtip, our only single desire is to do that which England expects of every man at such a crisis,—our duty, entirely irrespective of all personal considerations."

I wrung Bodwinkle's hand warmly (I could have crushed every bone in it), and threw an expression of tender interest into my glance as I said, "I wonder, Bodwinkle, how many candidates are actuated by these lofty views in the coming election; but you must not let yourself be too much carried away by your Quixotic convictions. Remember, my friend, what you owe to your party."

"I never forget it," said Bodwinkle, readily. "I have four things to consider—my country, my party, my family, and my conscience. I begin by asking my conscience what are the interests of my country. My conscience replies promptly that my party should be in power. I then ask my conscience what are the interests of my family, and my conscience invariably says the same thing. I then ask my conscience whether it has any political views of its own, and my conscience responds that it is a mercantile conscience, which has always been absorbed in commerce, and that takes no interest in abstract politics; so that practically, you see, I have no difficulty, so far as my conscience is concerned."

"Wog is right," I mused as I walked home—"*postiche* is everywhere. We certainly do 'make up' well. I suppose this country never looked more fair and flourishing in the eyes of the world in general than it does at this moment. We have made a great *succès* by means of *postiche*—there is no denying it. But we shall fall to pieces all of a sudden like old Lady Pimlico; and the wrinkles will appear before long in the national cheeks in spite of the rouge. Ah, the taunts we shall have to endure when the *postiche* is discovered, from the rivals that have always been jealous and are still under the prestige of our former charms! Then the kings of the earth with whom we have lived delicately will turn against us, for they will remember our greed and our pride and our egotism, in the days when we sold our virtue for gold, and our honour for a mess of pottage. Is there no one who will cry aloud in the streets while there is yet time?—will there not be one man in these coming elections who will have the courage to tell the people that their senses are so drugged by prosperity that they are blind to the impending doom, and that the only way to avert it will be by a policy diametrically opposed to that which has fascinated the nation for the last few years, because it has conducted them so pleasantly along those smooth and flowery paths that lead to destruction? Be sure, oh my countrymen, that for you collectively, as well as individually, there is a broad and a narrow way, and that as surely as a nation ignores its duties towards God and its obligations towards its neighbours, so surely will a swift judgment overtake it!" I was interrupted by a policeman at this point, who kindly called my attention to the fact that in my prophetic fervour I had myself been crying aloud in the streets, and accompanying my denunciations with appropriate action. "I will throw off a few of these ideas for the benefit of my constituents, while the sacred fire is still upon me," thought I, as I stood at my bay-window, and watched the grey dawn of the June morning breaking over Green Park. Sleep at such a moment is impossible, and I pulled the addresses of Spiffy and Bodwinkle from my pocket.

"Gentlemen," says Spiffy to the independent electors of Shuffleborough, "in soliciting the favour of your suffrages at the approaching general election, I am aware that I labour under the disadvantage of coming before you as an untried man, but I ask you all the more confidently on this account to substitute me for one who has been tried and found wanting. Still more painfully conscious am I of the fact that I am open to the charge of causing a fatal split in that Liberal party to which I have the honour to belong. Gentlemen, I regret to say that in some instances the members of that party have not been true to the principles which they profess, and have issued addresses almost identical in the terms they employ and in the measures they advocate with those of the Liberal Conservative party. It is no satisfaction to me to be told that there are as many false Conservatives as there are false Liberals. As a friend of the people I am opposed to all compromises, and will unflinchingly expose treachery in the camp. You will find that my political views are clear and decided.

"Though a member of the Church of England, I am in favour of the total abolition of Church-rates, as I believe that you will spiritualise the Church precisely in proportion as you starve it.

"I am in favour of an extension of the franchise to such an extent as will comprise all the working-classes, and thus pave the way to that universal suffrage in which I myself shall be included, and for the first time enjoy the privilege of voting.

"Should I fail to be returned as your member upon this occasion, I shall be in favour of a redistribution of seats.

"I believe that an era of universal peace is dawning upon the world, and I am therefore an advocate of the total suppression of our armaments both by sea and land.

"T think that the Christian spirit displayed in our foreign policy which has induced us to court national insult for the purpose of setting an example of forbearance, and which has enabled us humbly but surely to extend our commercial relations, has procured for us the highest moral position which has ever yet been accorded to a people. To increase the wealth of the nation and to foster its Christian spirit, will be recognised by me as a primary duty, if I am honoured with the high trust of being your representative in the Commons House of Parliament."

Now comes Bodwinkle's address, written by the versatile author of the last:—

"GENTLEMEN,—The appearance of a third candidate in the Liberal interest within the last few days induces me to break the silence which I have up to this time preserved. I have observed with pain that in many instances the addresses issued by gentlemen calling themselves Liberal Conservatives or Conservative Reformers, are of the most subversive tendency, and entirely opposed to the spirit of that old and enlightened party to which I have the honour to belong. I repudiate, therefore, entirely that temporising language which a large number of candidates calling themselves Conservatives hold, and which it has suited one of my opponents, who calls himself a Liberal, to adopt. I believe I shall best recommend myself to this constituency by an honest and unswerving advocacy of those views which the Tory party of this country have invariably maintained. More fondly attached, if possible, to the Church of England than I was upon the occasion when I last addressed you, I am more than ever convinced that money is the only thing that keeps it going. I am therefore entirely opposed to the abolition of those rates which form the foundation of that pillar upon which the State has been accustomed securely to repose.

"I am opposed to the enfranchisement of the working man, as, in the probable event of a combination between the labouring classes and the aristocracy, that middle class to which I have the honour to belong would cease to direct the destinies of the country. Any lateral measure of reform, unattended, however, by a vertical movement, which should exclude this possibility, will have my entire concurrence.

"I am in favour of a measure which shall largely increase the armaments of the country, and at the same time reduce the cost of their maintenance.

"I have profound confidence in the policy of the great Conservative party in their relations with foreign nations. The fact that they have hitherto declined to define what that policy is, renders it impossible for me to enter more fully into this subject at present.

"In a word, should you do me the honour to return me as your member, you will find me Liberal only in my views as to the modes in which money may be acquired, and Conservative always when there is a question of expenditure."

It is a grand idea but a great experiment this of having convictions, which Spiffy has just started, thought I. I have been cursed with them all my life, but never could turn them to account. Now in this case, for instance, he is using convictions—*postiche* convictions certainly—to get Bodwinkle into Parliament; the result of my convictions is, that if I express them they will turn me out. A prophet is without honour in his own country, more especially when the whole constituency has become sceptical and apathetic. I shall issue an address to the free and independent electors of Dunderhead. And under the inspiration of the moment I wrote as follows:—

"PICCADILLY, *June 20, 1865.*

"GENTLEMEN,—In announcing my intention not to solicit your suffrages at the approaching general election, I feel that it is due to you that I should state the reason why I do not again seek the high honour which you have upon two previous occasions conferred upon me, of representing you in Parliament. The prosperity of the country is now so great that I feel it has no further need of my services. In default of any great question of national importance, the rival political parties are reduced to the lamentable predicament of having nothing to fight for except office. As I have never taken the slightest interest in the fortunes of either party, except as embodying or representing the triumph of certain principles, the disappearance of those principles, and the difficulty of distinguishing by their expressed opinions between one party and the other, renders it quite impossible for me to follow the example of the candidates on both sides, and to stand upon—nothing! Gentlemen, I have no doubt that before very long something will turn up for me to stand upon. I will wait till then. Meantime, I feel that to profess any decided convictions upon matters either of home or foreign politics at this juncture would be considered in bad taste, if not impertinent, and I shall therefore reserve whatever I have to say for a future occasion, when the exigencies of the country may render it absolutely necessary that some individual in it should have an opinion."

There, I don't think I need say anything more. I meant to have written these Dunderheadians something that would have made them remember me after I was gone; but I am getting sleepy, and they would not have understood it. I will give £1000 to be applied to the wants of the municipality instead. "In conclusion," I went on, "I beg to offer a tribute to the only article of political faith in which you still believe, and to place £1000 at the disposal of the mayor and corporation, which, in addition to the money spent in the contest that my retirement will render inevitable, will, I trust, not only be of substantial service to the borough, but secure my re-election upon any future occasion.

"Frank Vanecourt."

Good-night, Dunderheadians. If in spite of this you send me a requisition to stand again, I will decline on a ground simple enough even for your comprehension—It is too hot!

It was no business of mine, after the explanation which I had had with Lady Ursula upon the subject of our rumoured engagement, to revert to the topic with any of her family. If Lady Broadhem was dissatisfied with the position of affairs, I supposed that I should hear of it quite soon enough; my only anxiety was about Ursula herself. I trembled for her domestic peace and comfort. Broadhem's few words about his sister's happiness under the altered circumstances were very significant, and I determined therefore to get her ladyship as much in my power as possible, by exercising to its utmost extent the right which I had wrung from her of a full control over her pecuniary affairs. If my wealth did not enable me to purchase my own happiness, it should at least enable me to secure the happiness of her whom I loved best in the world. I had never wavered in my resolution somehow or other to effect this great end, but my plans must of necessity undergo some change now that Lady Broadhem's eyes were opened to the real state of the case. I was much puzzled what to do about Grandon. Sometimes I felt a yearning to take him fully into my confidence and consult with him upon that delicate topic which touched us both so nearly; but though he was kind and considerate as ever, there was a constraint about our intercourse of which we were both painfully conscious. We avoided all allusion to the Broadhems, and he never called in Grosvenor Square, nor, so far as I know, had met Lady Ursula since the memorable dinner which had terminated so disagreeably for us all. Under the circumstances, I had also thought the wisest, and for many reasons the most proper, course for me was, to abstain from going there until I should hear from Lady Broadhem; and although I was anxious to consult her upon many business matters, I preferred letting them remain in abeyance to courting an interview which I dreaded. At last I began to think Lady Broadhem's silence rather ominous. I felt that a thunder-cloud had been gathering for some time past, and that the sooner it burst the better. I occasionally found myself walking past the door of the house, and wondering what was going on inside it. I felt that there would be something undignified about pumping Broadhem, and yet every time I met him I experienced an irresistible desire to do so.

At last one day he volunteered a remark, from which I gathered that he was as anxious for information as I was. "Have you seen my mother lately?" he began.

"Not for weeks."

"Do you know she is carrying on a lot of things just the same as ever?"

"I don't think that possible," I said; "she could do nothing without my knowledge."

"She is, though," said Broadhem; "I can't quite make out what is going on, because, you know, she never condescends to discuss her affairs with any of us; but I feel certain there is some new scheme afloat."

"Is she kind to your sister?" I asked.

"She is neither kind nor unkind: she is very little at home, and seems to have lost all interest in her own family. She wants us to believe that it is the heathen; but I must say that she never used to neglect her daughters for them, and always said, what so many good people forget, that the first duty of a Christian woman was to attend to her own family. I am getting very uneasy," said Broadhem, with a sigh; "I feel a presentiment that there is some sort of a crash coming; I wish you would go and see her."

"I did not intend going to her conversazione next week, but as she has sent me a card I suppose she wants to see me. I will come and hear my friend Joseph Caribbee Islands hold forth. By the way, I quite forgot I promised to ask Lady Broadhem for a card for Lady Wylde and her daughter; will you send one when you get home? You don't know Miss Wylde, do you?"

"Yes," said Broadhem, and he coloured and looked away; "I have just met her, and that is all. Did she ask you for the invitation?"

"What! you have met her, and she did not tell you the interest she takes in missions? I see you are half converted already. Take care, Broadhem; you are no great catch; but she does not, perhaps, exactly know that, and all is fish that comes to her net. Nevertheless, don't forget to send her the invitation;" and I saw the flush of gratified vanity mount to the brow of Broadhem, and no longer wondered why Wild Harrie had expressed a wish to make Lady Ursula's acquaintance. Poor Ursula! what Broadhem had said about his mother's change of manner decided me not to neglect the opportunity which presented itself of going to her "meeting," and coming to a distinct understanding with Lady Broadhem upon the present position of affairs. I had no doubt that that veteran campaigner had not been idle; and I was afraid, under the circumstances, that too much time had already been allowed her.

"Do you think Miss Wylde is going down to Ascot?" asked Broadhem, who had maintained an embarrassed silence during this interval.

"She went down yesterday with the Helters; she stays the week with them at their cottage," I replied.

"I have never been to Ascot," he said, awkwardly—"in fact I never saw a race in my life. I think a man, even though he does not approve of racing, ought to have seen it once—don't you?"

"Certainly," said I, "especially when you can see Wild Harrie at the same time."

"I say," said Broadhem, and he stopped short.

"Well?"

"I wish to goodness there was some way of going to Ascot without being seen. I suppose one is sure to come across a lot of men one knows."

"Not if you go and stay with the clergyman of the parish," I said.

"I don't know him. It is not for myself, but I don't think my mother would like my going."

"Then don't go."

"What an unsatisfactory fellow you are! I shall go and talk over the matter with Ursula—she always helps me out of my difficulties."

"What does she know about Ascot?" I asked.

"Oh, she does not know about Ascot, but somehow or other she always tells me what is the best thing to do about everything."

"I suppose, then, you tell her everything?"

"Almost," he said.

"Take my advice, and make a clean breast of it, my dear boy;" and I felt kindly towards him for the way he spoke about his sister. "Depend upon it, no half confidences do in such a case. Tell her that I shall come to you on Thursday of next week;" and I pressed his hand. I had never cared about him for his own sake, but my heart warmed towards him for hers.

PART VI.

THE "——."

PICCADILLY, *July 1.*

I am now about to venture upon the very thinnest ice upon which fool ever rushed. The fact is, I am morally trembling like an aspen; but somebody must do it. I have put it off for five months, and tried to work up my courage by hammering away at the fashionable world, but they take it like lambs. Dear people, whatever their vices may be, they never resent criticism. Whether their consciences tell them they are superior to it, or whether they have not got consciences, I don't know, but, on the whole, the fashionable world is an easy, good-natured world; but oh, not so that other world, which is still essentially "the world," and very necessary to keep unspotted from, though it is thankful that it is not as that other world is, from which in its humility it takes care to distinguish itself by the self-applied epithet of "religious." It grieves me to think of the number of my friends whom I shall pain by presuming to touch upon this subject, to say nothing of the righteous indignation I shall call down from those whose function it has been to give, not take, reproof. The great art of the "worldly-holies"—not, I believe, deliberately practised, but insensibly acquired—is to confuse in the minds of the poor dear "wholly-worldlies" the sublime religion which they profess, with their mode of professing it. So they would have it to be understood that, when you find fault with their practices, you are reflecting upon that very religion, the precepts of which they seem to some utterly to ignore. The "religious world" is no more composed of exclusively good men and women than the Episcopalian Church is. I will even venture to go further, and say that the good men and women in it are a very small minority, judging only from the public performances of the "worldly-holies" in matters in which humility, sincerity, self-sacrifice, and toleration, are concerned. And if you want a proof of it, ask your friends in the religious world if they agree in what I say of it, and the very few you may find who do, will be that small minority of whom I speak.

I am perfectly ready to admit that I have no more right to preach to them than they have to preach to me. I only ask those among them who are sincere, to believe that I am actuated by the same desire to improve them that they are to do good to me. It is not merely in their own interest, but in the interest of their fellow-men, that I venture to write thus, and to point out to them that, if they "lived the life," instead of talking the talk, they might attract instead of repelling that other world which they condemn. It is not living the life to form a select and exclusive society, with its vanities and its excitements, and its scandals and its envyings and jealousies, which keeps itself aloof from the worldly world, on the ground that it professes and represents a religion of love. Those who sit in Moses' seat are not on that account examples of the "life;" on the contrary, "whatsoever they bid you observe, that observe and do; but do not ye after their works, for they say and do not."

Above all, do not confound the Pharisee with the religion, or suppose that an attack on the one in any way implies irreverence towards the other. This is a very important distinction to make, as I am about to describe a religious entertainment at Lady Broadhem's with the religion left out, which will draw down upon me much odium. There is, in fact, no stronger proof of the force and despotic power of the Phariseeism of the present day, than the unpopularity which one incurs by attempting to expose it. Christians, in the real sense of the term, were always told to expect persecution and now, as in old time, the quarter from which it comes is the religious world. It is a hard saying, and one which, unfortunately, nobody has yet been found worthy to prove; but whenever he comes into this city of London, who can embody in himself the life and live it, he will be repudiated by the "worldly holies."

"The Countess of Broadhem requests the pleasure of Lord Frank Vanecourt's company at a conversazione on Thursday the 22d, at nine o'clock.

"The Bishop of the Caribbee Islands will give some account of the mission-work in his diocese."

That was the form of the card; and at nine punctually I responded to the invitation which it contained.

For the benefit of those of my readers who have never been admitted within the sacred precincts of the religious world, I should tell them that there is nothing in their outward appearance to distinguish them from the other world. The old ladies come in, followed by trains of daughters, furbelowed and flounced by the same dressmakers who clothe worldly people; but there is a greater variety of men—the older ones are often snuffy, and look unwashed. They constantly wear thick boots, and their black waistcoats are not embroidered, and button higher up, which gives them a more staid appearance. They are generally pervaded by an air of complacency and calm superiority, and converse in measured unctuous accents, checkered by beaming smiles when they are not contradicted. The youths, on the other hand, present in most cases an intellectually weak aspect. They are quite as much addicted to flirting with the young ladies as if they belonged to the other world, but want that hardihood, not to say impertinence, which characterises the lavender-gloved tribe who are still heathens. The arrangement of the room is somewhat that of a private concert, only instead of a piano is a table, behind which are seated Joseph Caribbee Islands, Chundango, and several other lay and clerical performers. In the centre of this table is a vase, which Joseph hopes to see filled with subscriptions before the proceedings terminate. There is a suspicion, however, that things may not go off quite smoothly, as a lay member present, who does a good deal of amateur preaching, intends to take him to task about certain unsound views which we knew our friend Joseph entertains. I am sorry to say that some of the young gentlemen leaning in the doorway, where I stand, anticipate this encounter with apparent satisfaction. Among them is Broadhem, who has never once taken his eyes off Wild Harrie. That young lady is more plainly dressed than anybody else in the room. Her hair is neatly and modestly drawn back. She might have risked a larger chignon, but she had never been to an entertainment of this kind before, and did not know how they dressed; her eyes are only now and then furtively raised, and she takes a quick glance round the room, winding up with Broadhem; and a twitching at the corners of her mouth makes me envy Amy Rumsort, who will, no doubt, receive a most graphic and embellished report of the whole affair. There is a good deal of murmuring and rustling and getting into places, and a few hardy men manage to squeeze themselves next the crinoline of their especial desire, and then they go on whispering and tittering to each other, till Joseph says in a very loud tone—Ahem!

On which a general silence. It seems as impossible and incongruous for me to write here what now takes place, as it did at the time to take part in it. It requires no stretch of imagination on the part of my readers to divine what movement it was which caused the next general rustle. Remember that a great proportion of these young ladies were brought here by their mammas, and in their secret souls would have rather been at a ball; but their mammas disapproved of balls, and made them do this instead. Now, tell me, which was most wrong? I knew of one young lady, at least, whose object in coming was not to do what she was then doing. How many young men would have been there had there been no young ladies? and what were they all thinking about now? And as I looked at the subscription-vase, and listened to the monotonous voice of a "dear Christian friend" behind it, who had been called upon to open the proceedings, I thought, Can it be possible that these are those of whom it is said, "they devour widows' houses, and for a pretence make long prayer"? Can it be possible to put anything into that vase without the right hand knowing what the left hand is doing, and all the people seeing both hands? Is not "the trumpet" even now being "sounded" by "the hypocrites" that they may have "glory of men"? Is there, in fact, any difference, practically, between kneeling in Lady Broadhem's drawing-room, by way of an after-dinner entertainment, and loving "to pray standing in the synagogues, and in the corners of the streets, that you may be seen of men"? Is there any part of a clergyman's dress called a phylactery; and if so, when he becomes a bishop, does the hem of it become broader? and if it was wrong for a priest in Jerusalem, eighteen hundred years ago, to be called "Rabbi, Rabbi," is it less wrong for one in London now to be called "My lord, My lord"?

I was thinking how much more usefully Bishop Colenso would have been employed in pointing out those anomalies in the practice of his religion, instead of the discrepancies in its records, and what a much stronger case the Zulu might have made out against Christians if he had known as much of the countries which they inhabit as I do, when the rustling again became general, and the monotonous voice ceased.

"Dear Christian friends," began Joseph—and here I may remark that this epithet is only applied by the worldly-holies to one another—one of the chief characteristics of those who belong to the religious world being constantly to talk as though they were a privileged few, a chosen flock, and as though that new commandment, "that ye love one another," was applicable only as among themselves, and consisted chiefly in addressing one another in affectionate and complimentary terms. Even these they withhold, not merely from the wholly-worldlies, but from those who differ from them upon all points of doctrine which they assume to be vital. Hence, by constantly toadying and flattering each other, they insensibly foster that description of pride which apes humility, and acquire that air of subdued arrogance which is so displeasing to society at large. So when Joseph said, "Dear Christian friends," there was clearly written on the self-satisfied faces of most of the audience, "that is the least you can say of us," or words to that effect.

Now let me in a little more detail tell who some of these friends were. The religious world in London being a very large and well-to-do world, they want religious lawyers, and religious bankers, and religious doctors; they like to get their wine from somebody who holds sound views, but I think they cease to be so particular about the principles of those from whom they get their bonnets.

However that may be about trades, the demand is immediately met in all the professions, and young men starting in life with a "connection" in the religious world must belong to it if they wish to succeed. This is another anomaly. In former times it involved stripes, persecution, poverty, and contumely to be a "Christian," but a "dear Christian friend" of the present day need be afraid of none of these things. He would never be called mad for making a profession of the views of the early Christians; but he would if, with a good religious opening in a professional point of view, he declined to take advantage of it. Then look what society it gets you into—you become a sort of brother; and, I am sorry to say, I know several young men who saw no chance of getting into the fashionable world, and who took to the other as a good introduction. In fact there was one standing in the doorway with me, the son of a solicitor I knew at Dunderhead, who was in the office of his uncle, who was Lady Broadhem's solicitor. Do you think either he or his uncle were sincere, or that he would have ever had the slightest chance of paying attention to Lady Bridget, which he positively had the presumption to do, if he had not enrolled himself in the band of "dear Christian friends"? He is a very good hand at the doctrine of love when the people to be loved are the aristocracy. He has just invited me on the part of his uncle to a conversazione, at which will be exhibited a converted Aztec, and at which that Christian solicitor, whose wife is a fat woman fanning herself in the front row, will positively induce the great majority of those now here, including a fair sprinkling of persons with titles, to be present.

Now far be it from me to imply that there are not earnest, sincere, and to some extent self-sacrificing, professors of the Christian religion, who I know will persist in mistaking me, and imagine that by writing this I bring the religion itself into contempt. I say again that those who bring it into the most contempt are those who profess it most, and that it is to counteract their prejudicial influence upon society that I venture to incur their animosity.

I shall not report Joseph's speech at length, still less attempt to follow Chundango in his unctuous remarks, in the course of which he lavished flattery upon his audience to an extent even beyond what they could bear; they swallowed it, however, with tea and ices, which were handed round, but I got so worked up at last by a smooth-faced man who was describing what he had gone through for the sake of the heathen, while he was living luxuriously in one of the most charming little mission establishments which I have ever visited, that I made the following remarks:—

"Ladies and Gentlemen,—When I came here this evening nothing was farther from my purpose than to address you. I cannot allow, however, the remarks of the Bishop of the Caribbee Islands, of Mr Chundango, or of the Rev. Mr Beevy, to pass unnoticed.

"The Bishop of the Caribbee Islands, in the course of the very graphic account which he has given you of the progress of conversion in his diocese, and of the number of interesting and instructive deathbeds which he has witnessed, has entered into a calculation by which it would appear that the average cost of the conversion of a human soul in those islands is a little over £6. Ladies, you pretend to believe that, but you don't. It would be impossible for you to sit there with strings of lost human souls round your necks, and what would keep an infant school in each ear, if you really believed that you could save a soul for £6. You come here and listen to gentlemen who give you an account of the sacrifices they make for the heathen, and of results which do not look so well on the spot as on paper; and because you throw a pound into that vase in the presence of the company, you think that you have done something for them too. 'They may give up all,' you say, 'but we can't afford to save more than two or three souls per annum.'

"Ladies and gentlemen, as far as my experience goes, you neither of you as a rule give up anything for the heathen. I cannot, therefore, share in your wonder at the barren results of your missionary efforts. The Tabernacle Missionary Society, for instance, offers to a young man of the lower middles" (Mr Beevy's father was a butcher, so I did not like to enter more fully into this part of the subject) "the opportunity of becoming a reverend and a gentleman, and thus advancing a step in society. It gives him £300 a-year to begin with, £80 a-year more with his wife, £20 a-year with his first child, and £10 a-year with each succeeding olive-branch. It educates these free of expense at Holloway, and it pays an indefinite number of passages between England and the 'mission-field,' according as the health of the family requires it; and permit me to say that, if to receive between £400 and £500 a-year in a tolerable climate, with a comfortable house rent-free, and the prospect of a pension at the end, is to give up all for the heathen, I have myself made the experiment without personal discomfort. Perhaps I speak with a certain feeling of bitterness on this subject, for I cannot forget that upon one occasion while residing among the heathen, a gentleman who is now present, and who had sacrificed his all for them, outbid me for a horse at an auction after I had run him up to sixty guineas. With such a magnificent institution as this for supplying 'purse' and 'scrip,' and for 'taking thought for the morrow' in the way of pensions, &c., tell me honestly whether you think you deserve real, not nominal conversions? You have instituted a sort of 'civil service,' with which 'you compass sea and land to make one proselyte.' You go to him with a number of bibles, Armstrong guns, drunken sailors, and unscrupulous traders, a combination which goes to make up what you call 'civilisation,' and you wonder that your converts are actuated by the same motive which my own Hindoo servant once told me induced him to leave his own religion, in which he could not venture to get drunk, and become a Christian.

"Do you think it is the fault of the religion that you don't make converts, or the fault of the system under which it is propagated? If you gave up 'the enticing words of man's wisdom,' and tried a little of 'the demonstration of the spirit and of power,' don't you think the result would be different? If you are only illumined by 'a dim religious light' yourselves, how do you expect to dissipate the gross darkness of paganism? You have only got an imitation blaze that warms nobody at home, and you wonder when you take it abroad that it leaves everybody as cold and as dead as it finds them.

"My dear Christian friends, in the face of the living contradiction which we all present in our conduct to the religion we profess, our missionaries can only convince the heathen of the truth of Christianity by living the life upon which that religion is based, by means of which it can alone be powerful, and which is only now not lived by Christians, because, as was prophesied, there is no 'faith on the earth.' I have spoken to you faithfully, even harshly, but, believe me, I have done so in a spirit of love. If you can take it in the same spirit, I shall feel I have done you a great injustice."

I was so excited while delivering myself of these observations that I was quite unconscious of the effect I was producing. I remember there was a deathlike silence, and that when I sat down the gentlemen behind the table looked flushed and agitated. Mr Beevy first rose to reply to observations which, he said, reflected upon him personally, no less than upon the society to which he was proud to say he belonged. He then explained the circumstances under which he had been induced to give £65 for the horse; and retaliated upon me in language which I will spare my readers now, as they will see it in the 'Discord,' when that organ of the "worldly-holies" does me the honour to review this veracious history. The religious world has a more choice catalogue of epithets for their enemies than any other section of the community. I need not therefore suggest "ribald" as appropriate to the present occasion. It was the term applied to me by the amateur lay-preacher after Mr Beevy sat down. Finally, the proceedings terminated in some confusion; before they did, however, I rose again to point out how completely the conduct of those present had proved my case—either the faults to which I alluded existed, and there was nothing more to be said; or I had buffeted them without cause, and they had *not* "taken it patiently," a course of conduct quite inexcusable in a meeting composed exclusively of dear Christian friends. If there is a thing I yearn for, it is the love of my fellow-men. By making the "worldly-holies" consider me an enemy, I ought to secure an unusual share of their affection. Remember, now, if you abuse me for this, it is unchristian; if you leave me alone, you will be treating me "with the contempt I deserve," and that is unchristian too; the right thing for you to do is to take the charitable view, to admit that my motives may be good, even if the means employed are injudicious. When I am abruptly asked in an omnibus, by an entire stranger, who may happen to belong to the "straitest sect," the most solemn question which one man can put to another, I do not resent it. I believe he is sincerely trying to "awaken me" with a "word in season." I question the taste, but I respect the motive. Do the same to me, dear friends. We are all bad, and I am far worse than any of you; but still I may show how bad the best of us are. By living in a fool's paradise here, we shall not qualify ourselves for the other one to come. Depend upon it, we are all a great deal too comfortable to be safe.

"Lord Frank," said Lady Broadhem while Joseph was emptying the vase and pocketing the contents, and the rest of the world was beginning to circulate, "had I known that your object in coming here this evening was to insult my guests, I certainly should not have asked you."

"You do me an injustice, Lady Broadhem," I said. "Nothing was further from my purpose when I came here this evening than to have said anything. I supposed by your sending me the card that you wanted to see me, and came; but my conscience would not allow me to remain silent under the circumstances."

"Nothing can justify such conduct," said her ladyship, more angry than I had ever seen her. "I cannot say how truly grateful I am that it is all at an end between you and Ursula;" and Lady Broadhem shuddered at the idea of having exhibited myself as I had done, if I had been her son-in-law.

"It was to show you what an escape you had made, and reconcile you to the disappointment, that I expressed my sentiments so strongly," I said maliciously. All my better nature seemed to leave me as I found myself involved in a fresh encounter with this woman, who certainly possesses the art of raising my devil beyond any one I ever met.

"I can't talk to you now," said Lady Broadhem, who did not wish to be too manifestly discovered without her Christian spirit, though there was not much of it left in anybody in the room. "I see Mr Beevy coming this way, and to avoid any unpleasantness you had better not stay any longer just now. Come to-morrow at twelve;" and she intercepted the missionary as he was advancing towards me with a somewhat truculent air. All this time I had seen, but not had an opportunity of exchanging a word with Ursula, who occupied an obscure corner, and seemed anxious to attract as little notice as possible. I made my way to her now. She looked careworn and nervous.

"I am afraid your remarks do not seem to have given satisfaction, Lord Frank," she said; "and if I may venture to say so, I think you might have said what you did in language less calculated to give offence. I quite agreed with you in the main, but do you think you will do good by thrusting truths home with little ceremony?"

"I caught the habit from the class I was attacking, I suppose. They seldom realise the harm they do by their disagreeable mode of inculcating precepts they don't practise, and they never get preached to, though they listen to sermons twice every Sunday."

"But don't you think you fairly lay yourself open to the charge of presumption in thus taking to task men who have made theology their study, and in condemning a whole set of people, who, if they occasionally are indiscreet, are most of them sincere, and certainly do a great deal of good? Are you sure your own religious opinions are sufficiently formed to warrant you in commenting so strongly on the views of others?"

"I don't comment on their views, but on their conduct. While we are not to judge others, we are also told that by their fruits we shall know them. It does not require a profound knowledge of the dogmas of a creed to perceive the effect it has upon those who profess it. Fortunately I have thought for myself, and have come at last firmly to believe in the religion, but I should never have done so had I continued to judge of it by its professors."

"Then you think the form in which Christianity is professed and practised prejudices the cause of true religion?" said Lady Ursula.

"I have not a doubt of it. Our friends here 'bind heavy burdens and grievous to be borne, and lay them on men's shoulders, but they themselves will not move them with one of their fingers.' If you will substitute charitable bazaars for races, oratorios for operas, conversaziones like this for balls, and otherwise conform to the 'letter' which they have established, they accept you as a brother, but there is very little difference in the 'spirit' which pervades the so-called religious, and that which pervades the worldly excitements. The 'mint, anise, and cummin' are there; but the 'judgment' is perverted, the 'mercy' limited, and the 'faith' barren. However, we are getting into rather too theological a discussion, and Broadhem looks as if he was anxious to interrupt us."

"I think he is quite happy where he is," replied Lady Ursula. "You know Miss Wylde, whom he got mamma to ask here to-night, don't you?"

"A little. By the way, did he go down to Ascot after all, and did he tell you the especial motive he had in view?"

"Yes, I recommended him to go, as I think he is too much accustomed to walk in the groove in which he has always found himself, and as I do not see much difference, in a matter of that kind, between wanting to go and going. He came back thoroughly dissatisfied, having failed to do more than exchange a few words with Miss Wylde, by whom he seems quite infatuated. Can you tell me something about her?"

I gave Ursula an account of Wild Harrie, based on Spiffy's information, not very flattering, I am afraid, to that young lady, and wound up with something about putting Broadhem on his guard.

"I don't quite agree with you there," she replied; "opposition will not improve matters in his case, and you must forgive me for not taking the unfavourable view of Miss Wylde's character that you have given me. I really think Broadhem has, for the first time in his life, fallen in love, and the best way to take care of him will be to know intimately the lady of his choice, so I shall interrupt their *tête-à-tête* with the view of cultivating Miss Wylde."

"But what will Lady Broadhem say to such an alliance? Miss Wylde has not got a farthing."

"I don't think he need anticipate any opposition from mamma,—at all events not just now," said Lady Ursula, with a sigh, and I knew there was a secret grief which she could not tell hidden in her words. "I am so glad that Broadhem is above the consideration of money, and has really allowed himself to be carried away by his feelings, that I feel quite grateful to Miss Wylde, and inclined to love her already."

"I think they are going to commence operations of some sort again," I said, as I saw the enemies I love, but who don't return the affection, ranging themselves behind the table; "part two is about to begin, so I shall make my escape. Perhaps I shall see you to-morrow; I am coming to call on Lady Broadhem," and I left Lady Ursula, and had to squeeze past Broadhem and Wild Harrie. "You seem interested," I said to the latter, "as you are going to stay."

"I suppose you don't intend to show any more sport, Lord Frank, as you are going, so the best of the fun is over. I was just telling Lord Broadhem how I enjoyed that brilliant burst of yours; it was worth anything to watch the expressions on the countenances of all our friends here who have 'given up the world,' and who thought they were having it all their own way till you got up. I want Lord Broadhem to follow your lead, but it seems he considers himself 'a dear Christian friend.' We must break him of that, mustn't we? It is a very bad 'form.' I suppose you don't know what that expression means," Wild Harrie went on, her eyes dancing with mischief as she turned to Broadhem.

The struggles which that young gentleman's conscience was having with his affections were manifestly portrayed on his countenance, and Wild Harrie evidently was amusing herself by shocking his feelings. I must do her the justice to say that I don't think she could play the hypocrite if she tried; and I began to hope, as I looked at her frank reckless face, that her sins were more on the surface than in the heart. "I suppose you mean a form of worship," said Broadhem; "I wish you would not talk in this way. Whenever I try to have a little serious conversation with you, you turn it off with a joke. I must say," he added, sententiously, "that the style of young ladies' conversation in the present day is open to great improvement."

"I tell you what, Lord Broadhem," she retorted, "we will put each other through a course of training; you shall improve my conversation and 'style of going' generally, while I try to bring you into a little harder condition than you are at present. You have no idea of his innocence, Lord Frank, considering that he is a rising statesman upon whom the hopes of the Liberal party are fixed. I asked him just now, apropos of the speech he threatens us with, 'if he felt fit,' and he blushed to that degree that I felt quite shy. There was no harm in my saying that, was there?"

"None that I know of," said I; "but we are attracting general attention by talking so loud. Good-bye, Miss Wylde. I am afraid I must disturb you, Broadhem; your sister can't hear where she is, and wants your place;" and I walked off the young gentleman, to Wild Harrie's disgust, and saw with satisfaction that Lady Ursula took his vacated seat.

"What a curious thing it is," said Broadhem, "that I should find in Miss Wylde something which is to me so attractive! I daresay you think it odd my taking you so much into my confidence; but, except Ursula, I have no one to whom I can speak openly, and it is such a relief sometimes."

"On these occasions specially," said I.

"Do you know, I think that if I had her all to myself I could cure her faults, for I am quite alive to them. Don't you think there is something very fresh and natural about her?"

"Fresh, certainly, in what she would call the 'skittish' sense. As for the natural part of it, I should require to know her better before giving my opinion."

"You know," he went on, "she is the last person in the world with whom I imagined it possible I could have been in love: she says the most dreadful things sometimes—and I am afraid they amuse me more than they should; there is no doubt about her being immensely clever, but she is quite taken up with the world as yet."

"Not more than you are, my dear Broadhem; come and walk home with me: you will be back in time to put the Wyldes into their carriage, and I want to speak to you." I led him unresistingly to his coat and hat in the hall, and braved the stern gaze of a butler who apparently dressed after Mr Beevy, and who, when I arrived, had smiled blandly upon me as being 'one of us,' for all the servants in Lady Broadhem's establishment were guaranteed converted. "No servants, whose principles are not strictly Evangelical, and who are unable to produce unexceptionable testimony as to their personal piety, need apply"—that was the form of the advertisement, and the consequence was, that every menial in the house had brought a certificate of his or her entire change of heart from their last place. Lady Broadhem was also very particular about the theological views of the family they had just left.

The butler frowned severely upon me now, for he had been standing in the doorway with the curaçoa when I was addressing the meeting, no doubt sympathising keenly with Mr Beevy (I found out afterwards that Lady Broadhem was educating his son for the "work"), and said to Broadhem, "Does her ladyship know you are going away, my lord?"

"No," said Broadhem, with some hesitation; "I don't think she does. I am coming back again soon."

"I think, my lord, I shall have to let her ladyship know—perhaps your lordship will wait. James, mind the door." This meant that James was not to open it.

"Stop, my friend," I said; "your conscience tells you that you should not be a party to this irregularity on the part of his lordship,—is not that so?" I asked.

"Yes, my lord," said the butler, rigidly.

"I will accompany you to Lady Broadhem, then, to explain the circumstances. Be good enough to follow me," and I led the way up-stairs.

Now it so happens that I have a remarkable faculty of remembering faces, and I had been conscious for some weeks past of being familiar with the particularly ill-favoured countenance of Lady Broadhem's butler; but it was not until now that the circumstances under which I had first seen it flashed upon me. Not many years have elapsed since I achieved considerable renown in Australia as an amateur hunter of bushrangers. The sport exhilarated me, combining, as it did, an exciting physical with a wholesome moral exercise. I now remembered distinctly having caught Lady Broadhem's butler with a lasso. Indeed I had good reason not to forget it, for a shot he fired at me at the moment killed my favourite horse. That he should have failed to recognise in Lord Frank Vanecourt the notorious Mr Francis who had been the means of capturing not only himself, but a good many of his fraternity, was not wonderful. The discovery tickled me, and restored my good temper, which had been slightly ruffled.

"What a delightful change you must find it to be in the society of all these good people after having passed so many years in the bush!" I said, and my tone of anger suddenly became one of easy familiarity, as I turned sharply upon him, and, leaning against the banisters, benevolently scanned his distorted physiognomy. The play of his facial muscles, and changes of hue, interested me, so I continued—"But I will venture to say that you have never since paid such attention to any sermon as you did to mine that Sunday morning when I had you and your seven friends strapped to eight trees in a semicircle, and concluded my remarks, you may remember, with a few strokes of 'practical application.' I should like to hear the story of your escape from prison."

"Oh, my lord," he groaned, and his teeth chattered and his knees trembled, "I'm a reformed character—I am indeed. Perhaps if your lordship would kindly please to walk this way," and he opened a side door off the landing. "Knowing your lordship's generosity, and your lordship's interest in the family, and my own unworthiness, your lordship wouldn't be too hard upon a poor man whose repentance is genuine, and I could tell your lordship something of the very highest importance to her ladyship, and to Lady Ursula, and to your lordship, and to the whole family."

I knew the man to be a clever scoundrel, and saw that he evidently had some information which might prove of value. A mystery did exist—of that I had had abundant evidence. Was I justified in refusing to find the key?—besides, if this man really possessed some secret, could it be in more dangerous hands? This last consideration decided me, and I followed the returned convict to a little sanctum of his own, which opened off the pantry, from which I emerged five minutes later a wiser if not a better man.

"What a time you have been!" said Broadhem. "I suppose you have been arguing the point with my mother?"

"No, I left that to Drippings here." I did not know his name, but my spirits were high, and I gave him the first my imagination suggested. "You have no idea what a treasure your mother has got in this man. I assure you there is no knowing what you may not owe to the influence for good of one devoted Christian servant of this kind—the proof of it is, as you see, that Lady Broadhem is perfectly willing that you should do what you like for the rest of the evening. Good-night, Drippings," and I passed the bewildered James, who evidently thought that both I and the terrified-looking butler had gone suddenly mad.

"Broadhem," said I, "I have hit upon an entirely new and original idea. I am thinking of trying it myself, and I want you to try it too."

"Well," said Broadhem, "I am never surprised at anything you say or do; what is it?"

"It has been suggested to me by what I have seen at your mother's this evening—and you may depend upon it there is a great deal to be said in its favour; it is an odd thing it has not occurred to anybody before, but that leaves all the better opening for you and me."

"Go on," said Broadhem, whose curiosity was getting excited.

"Don't be in a hurry; it is possible you may not like the idea when you hear it, and under no circumstances must you tell it to anybody."

"All right," said Broadhem, "but I hope it has nothing to do with companies—I hate dabbling in companies. I believe one does more harm to one's name by making it common than one gets good through the money one pockets."

"Well, there is more truth than elegance of expression in that remark: it needs not have to do with companies unless you like."

"Now, if it has anything to do with politics, I am your man."

"You would make a great *coup* in politics with it; it is especially adapted for politics, and has never been tried."

"You don't say so," said Broadhem, delighted; "don't go on making one guess as if it was a game. Has it anything to do with the suffrage?"

"It has to do with everything," I said; "I don't think I can do it myself; I made a lamentable failure just now by way of a start," and I paused suddenly—"Who am I," I thought, "that I should venture to preach? What act have I done in life which should give weight to my words?" but the fervour was on me, and I could no more check the burning thoughts than the trumpet can control the sound it emits.

"Well," he said impatiently.

"LIVE THE LIFE."

"I don't understand you," said Broadhem.

"If you did," I said, "do you suppose I should feel my whole nature yearning as it is? What better proof could I desire that the life has yet to be lived than that you don't understand me? Supposing, now, that you and I actually put into practice what all these friends of your mother profess, and, instead of judging people who go to plays, or play croquet on Sunday, or dance, we tried to live the *inner* life ourselves. Supposing, in your case, that your own interest never entered your head in any one thing you undertook; supposing you actually felt that you had nothing in common with the people around you, and belonged neither to the world of publicans and sinners, nor to the world of scribes and Pharisees, but were working on a different plane, in which self was altogether ignored—that you gave up attempting to steer your own craft any longer, but put the helm into other hands, and could complacently watch her drive straight on to the breakers, and make a deliberate shipwreck of every ambition in life,—don't you think you would create rather a sensation in the political world? Supposing you could arrive at the point of being as indifferent to the approval as to the censure of your fellow-men, of caring as little for the highest honours which are in their power to bestow now, as for the fame which posterity might award to you hereafter; supposing that wealth and power appeared equally contemptible to you for their own sakes, and that you had no desire connected with this earth except to be used while upon it for divine ends, and that all the while that this motive was actuating you, you were striving and working and toiling in the midst of this busy world, doing exactly what every man round you was doing, but doing it all from a different motive,—it would be curious to see where you would land—how you would be abused and misunderstood, and what a perplexity you would create in the minds of your friends, who would never know whether you were a profound intriguer or a shallow fool. How much you would have to suffer, but what a balance there would be to the credit side! For instance, as you could never be disappointed, you would be the only free man among slaves. There is not a man or woman of the present day who is not in chains, either to the religious world or the other, or to family or friends, and always to self. Now, if we could get rid of the bonds of self first, we could snap the other fetters like packthread. What a grand sensation it would be to expand one's chest and take in a full, free, pure breath, and uplift the hands heavenward that have been pinioned to our sides, and feel the feeble knees strong and capable of enabling us to climb upwards! With the sense of perfect liberty we should lose the sense of fear, no man could make us ashamed, and the waves of public opinion would dash themselves in vain against the rock upon which we should then be established. The nations of the earth are beating the air for freedom, and inventing breech-loaders wherewith to conquer it, and they know not that the battlefield is self, and the weapons for the fight not of fleshly make. Have you ever been in an asylum for idiots, Broadhem?" I asked, abruptly.

"No," he said, timidly.

"Then you are in one now. Look at them; there is the group to which you belong playing at politics. Look at the imbecile smile of gratified vanity with which they receive the applause that follows a successful hit. That poor little boy has just knocked a political tobacco-pipe out of Aunt Sally's mouth, and he imagines himself covered with a lasting glory. There is another going to try a jump: he makes a tremendous effort before he gets to the stick, but balks, and carries it off in his hand with a grin of triumph. Look, there is a man with a crotchet; he keeps on perpetually scratching his left ear and his right palm alternately, and then touching the ground with the tips of his fingers. He never varies the process. Look at the gluttons who would do nothing but eat if they were allowed, like men who have just got into office, and see how spiteful they are, and what faces they make at each other, and how terribly afraid they are of their masters, and how they cringe for their favour, and how naughty they are when their backs are turned. Look, again, at these groups drawing, and carpentering, and gardening, imagining that they are producing results that are permanently to benefit mankind; but they are drawing with sticks, and carpentering with sham tools, and planting stones. And see, there is a fire-balloon going up; how delighted they all are, and how they clap their hands as the gaudy piece of tissue-paper inflated with foul gas sails over their heads. Is there one of the noisy crowd that knows what its end will be or that thinks of tomorrow? Is there one of them, I wonder, that suspects he is an idiot? If you find out, Broadhem, that you are not one of them, they will call you an idiot—be prepared for that. The life of a sound and sane man in such company cannot be pleasant. Every act of it must be an enigma to those around him. If he is afraid of them, they will turn and rend him; if he is fearless, they will hate him, because 'he testifies of the evil.' His life will be a martyrdom, but his spirit will be free, his senses new-born; and think you he would exchange the trials and labours which his sanity must entail upon him for the drivelling pleasures which he has lost? Tell me, Broadhem, what you think of my idea?"

"It is not altogether new to me, though I did not exactly understand what you meant at first," said Broadhem, who spoke with more feeling than I gave him credit for possessing. "I have never heard it put in such strong language before, but I have seen Ursula practise it, and I was wondering all the time you were talking whether you did."

"I never have yet," I said. "I began by telling you that the idea only occurred to me lately in its new form. I had often thought of it as a speculation. I began by assuming that purely disinterested honesty might pay, because an original idea well applied generally succeeds; but when I came to work the thing out, I found that there was a practical difficulty in the way, and that you could not be unselfish from a selfish motive a bit more than you could look like a sane man while you were really still an idiot. And so the fact is, I have talked the notion out to you as it has been suggested to me, though Drippings nearly drove it out of my head. I think the reason I felt impelled to do so was, that had it not been for your sister I should never have thought upon such subjects as I do now. I know her love for you, and the value of her influence over you. Even now she is devoting herself to guarding your interests in the most important step of a man's life, and I seem instinctively to feel how I can best please her. Don't you think she agrees in what I have said to-night, and would approve of the conversation we have had?"

"Yes," said Broadhem. "Do you know you are quite a different sort of fellow from what I imagined. I always thought that you did not believe in anything."

"That was because I lived exactly like my neighbours, without adding to my daily life the sin of professing belief in a religion to which it was diametrically opposed. Most of the sceptics of the present day are driven to their opinions by their consciences, which revolt against the current hypocrisy and glaring inconsistencies that characterise the profession of the popular theology. As a class I have found them honester, and in every way better men than modern Christians."

"Do you know why?"

"No," said Broadhem.

"Because modern Christians don't really believe much more than sceptics—a man's life is the result of his internal, not his external belief. There can be no life separate from internal belief, and the lives of men are imperfect because their belief is external. The right thing believed the right way must inevitably produce the perfect life. Either, then, the civilised world believes the wrong thing, or it believes the right thing the wrong way. In other words, faith and charity are inseparable, and when one is perfect the other is too. That is what I mean by 'living the life.'"

"According to that, you would make out that nobody rightly believes the Christian religion who is not perfect; that, you know, is ridiculous," said Broadhem.

"That is, nevertheless, exactly what I do mean. To know the doctrine, it is necessary to do the will. Christians of the present day adopt certain theological dogmas intellectually and call them their religious belief. This has a superficial and varying influence upon their lives, for it consists merely of opinions which are liable to change. The only kind of faith which is inseparable from life is a divine conviction of truth imparted to the intellect through the heart, and which becomes as absolute to the internal conscience as one's existence, and as impossible of proof. It may be added to, but what has once been thus accepted can never be changed. Such a faith cannot be selfish, for it has been derived from the affections, hence the life must be charitable. But the modern Christian belief, received by an effort of pure reason directly through the intellect, is not a divine intuition, which, if embodied, would result in a perfect life and a united Church, but a theological problem which professors of religion, unlike professors of mathematics, are at liberty to solve for their own benefit, according to their own taste, and to quarrel about incessantly, thereby giving occasion to the thoughtless to scoff, and to the thoughtful to reject all revelation as 'foolishness'—since it is incapable of demonstration by the Baconian method,—the only one known to these 'wise and prudent' philosophers, but one by which, fortunately for them, 'babes' are not expected to prove their relationship before believing in their mothers."

"Then," said Broadhem, "you actually mean to say that the whole of Christendom is wanting in this faith?"

"I fear that almost universally they mistake a bare belief for faith. Their theology thus becomes an *act* of memory instead of a rule of life, and Christianity is reduced to a superstition. The only way of distinguishing superstition from true religion is by an examination of results. But where are the fruits of modern Christianity? If it be absolutely true, and all-sufficient for purposes of regeneration, how am I to account for the singular fact that there is as much wickedness in London in the year 1865 A.D., as there was in Jerusalem in the year 1 B.C.? If the object of the last revelation was to take the place of the one before it, and to reform the world, why are the best modern Christians of my acquaintance no holier than the best modern Jews whom I have the honour to know?"

"But the object of the last revelation was not to reform the world, but to save it," he replied.

"Thanks, Broadhem, for having put in rather too epigrammatic a form, perhaps, to please those who believe it, the most diabolical sophism that was ever invented to beguile a Church—the doctrine that men can be saved by opinion without practice: that a man's practice may be bad, and yet because his faith is good his salvation is sure—that he can, by such a miserable philosophy as would disgrace the justice of the earth, escape the just sentence to be passed upon all his deeds. The results of so fatal a dogma must be a Church that tends to atheism, and that loves corruption. There is in every heart a something that speaks against this, and speaks with a burning language that sweeps the invisible chords of the inmost consciousness, and awakens a torrent of indignant denial of the shallow sophistry that a man can be saved if his thoughts and life are bad. If he cherish self-love, and the love of ruling others, though he intrench the intellect in the midst of all creeds, and span the reason with all faiths, making a sacred public profession before all men, he but adds to the heinousness of his crime, and makes more terrible the fast-coming and final judgment."

Broadhem stopped suddenly in the street as I finished in a somewhat excited tone, and gasped rather than spoke, "Frank, you literally astound me. I could never have believed it possible you would have come out in that line. Are those your own ideas or another's?"

"Another's," I replied, coolly. "I believe they are rather unsound, but I commend them to your notice, because, if they are not correct, Christianity will soon cease to exist, even in name; but if they are, then it contains within it a regenerating power hitherto undeveloped, whereby the world may be absolutely reformed. I will venture to assert that Christian nations will make no moral progress so long as they continue to cherish the pagan superstition that religion consists in trying to save themselves by virtue of a creed, instead of in trying to save others by the virtues of a life."

"But that's works," said Broadhem.

"Yes," I repeated, "that's works, but of a kind only possible when accompanied by intuitive living faith, which I have just endeavoured to describe. There is a promise that 'greater works than these shall they do' who 'believe.' Why, I want to know, have these 'works,' greater than any that were then accomplished, and which would reform the world, never been attempted? Because people don't believe in the tremendous power of disinterestedness, and they can't face the severe training which the perfection of self-sacrifice involves. So one set of 'worldly-holies' regard all personal discipline as a tempting snare to be avoided, and entertain a great horror of what they conceitedly term 'their own merits.' This very superfluous sentiment, combined with a selfish belief in certain doctrinals (of which they usually do make a merit), is enough, they imagine—the 'works' will follow; and so they do, and take the form we have just seen in your mother's drawing-room. Another set delight in a mild æsthetic sort of training, to be performed in a particular costume, according to the obsolete ceremonial rules of a Church 'which is divided against itself,' and their works take the fatuous form of ecclesiastical high art. Others, again, go to a still further extreme, and consider discipline not the means but the end. Hence they go through their drill in seclusion, exclusively for their own benefit, and their works take the form of scourgings and horse-hair shirts, and other mortifications of the flesh, which do no good to themselves nor to anybody else. And then, in strong contrast, are those who train enough in all conscience with 'gloves,' single-stick, sculls, and all suchlike appliances, and whose works take the form of tubbing, volunteering, and a general jovial philanthropy. I am not sure that they are not the most hopeful set after all; they believe in severe muscular training as necessary to produce great physical results. Get them to accept, the possibility of the world's regeneration by a divinely-directed effort of heroic spiritual discipline on the part of its inhabitants, and you might convert them from 'physical' into 'moral force' Christians. They understand the efficacy of 'a long pull, and a strong pull, and a pull all together;' and they might be shown that the real place for a 'biceps' is the will, not the arms; and instead of a body 'as hard as nails,' the chief aim of one's life should be to bring one's spirit to that condition—'hard,' be it understood, in the sense of being impervious to the influences which weaken and demoralise it—hard in its resistance to the tyranny of society, to the claims of family or friends, and to the force of 'natural' ties, where any of these things interfere with the 'spiritual' training. It is only by thus remaining in the world, and yet refusing to concede a jot to it upon any pretence, however plausible, that it is possible to acquire the internal isolation and strength of will necessary to the achievement of 'these greater works.' Depend upon it, the task of performing them is not hopeless because it seems stupendous. There are spiritual forces now latent in humanity powerful enough to restore a fallen universe; but they want to be called into action by fire. They are in a cold fluid state, and must be turned into stone. Sublime moment! when, conscious of the Titanic agency within them, and burning with desire to give it expression, men first unite to embody, and then with irresistible potency to impart to others that 'Life' which is 'the Light of men.'"

As I was thus speaking, we turned into Piccadilly, and an arm was passed through mine.

"Why is it," asked Broadhem, "that men are not yet at all conscious of possessing this spiritual agency?"

"Why is it, ask you?"—and the clear solemn voice of my new companion startled Broadhem, who had not seen him join me, so that I felt his arm tremble upon mine. "Ask rather why sects are fierce and intolerant; why worship is formal and irreverent; why zealots run to fierce frenzies and react to atheistic chills; why piety is constrained and lifeless, like antique pictures painted by the old Byzantines upon a golden ground; why Puseyism tries to whip piety to life with scourges, and starve out sin with fasts; why the altar is made a stage where Ritualists delight a gaping crowd, and the pulpit a place where the sleek official drones away the sleepy hour; why religious books are the dullest; why the clergyman is looked upon by the millions as a barrel-organ, whom the sect turns like the wandering Savoyard, unable to evolve a free-born note. There is but one answer——" and he stopped abruptly.

"What is it?" I said, timidly, for I was overwhelmed by the torrent of his eloquence.

"We have lost our God! That is why men are unconscious of His force within them. It is a terrible thing for a nation to lose its God. History shows that all nations wherein the religious inspiration has gone down beneath formalism, infidelity, a warlike spirit, an enslaving spirit, or a trading spirit, have burst like so many gilded bubbles, most enlarged and gorgeous at the moment of their close. Think of the old Scripture, 'The wicked shall be turned into hell, and all the nations that forget God.'"

"Who is that?" whispered Broadhem. "I never saw him before."

"I want to be alone with him," I replied. "Good night, Broadhem. You had better go back now, or you will find your friends gone. Think over what I have said. Once realise the '*mystery* of godliness,' and the martyrdom which it must entail will lose its terrors."

"Let him sacrifice us if He will," said he who had before spoken. "The true man is but a cannon-shot, rejoicing most of all when the Divine Artillerist shall send him irresistible and flaming against some foeman of the race risen from Pandemonium. Man—the true man—is like the Parthian's arrow, kindling into fiery flames as it leaves the bow. Man—the true man—is the Spirit-sword, but the sword-arm is moved by the heart of the Almighty."

Ah Piccadilly! hallowed recollections may attach to those stones worn by the feet of the busy idiots in this vast asylum, for one sane man has trodden them, and I listened to the words of wisdom as they dropped from the lips of one so obscure that his name is still unknown in the land, but I doubted not who at that moment was the greatest man in Piccadilly.

CONCLUSION.

MORAL.

PICCADILLY, *July 15.*

It will be seen by the date at which I am writing this, that I have been compelled to increase the pace I have been keeping up during the season. The fact is, my episode, like those of my neighbours, seems likely to be prematurely concluded by the course of political events, which will no doubt act prejudicially this year upon the happiness of many interesting members of society. Towards the close of the London season it is only natural that everything should culminate; but generally the actors in the scenes of real life so calculate that the curtain falls just at the right moment; or rather, that they shall be doing just the right thing when the curtain falls. The artists insensibly group themselves for the *grand tableau*. All over the stage episodes are occurring, any one of which taken separately would make a good sensation finale. There are wily mothers and desperate daughters throwing with unerring aim their nets over youths who have become reckless or imbecile. And there are unprincipled poachers setting snares for the pretty game they hope to destroy. Look at the poor victims, both male and female, trying to get disentangled. What a rush, and shuffle, and conflict of feelings and affections it is! The hearts that for the first time feel they have been touched as the moment of separation draws near; the "histories" which in all future time will form the most marked page in his or her life, and which have begun and ended in the season; the intimacies that have been formed, and which are to last for ever; those that have been broken; the fatal friendships which have been cemented this year, and the disastrous results of which, suspected on neither side, we shall read of in the newspapers years to come. What a curious picture would be the mind of London society if we could photograph it in February, and how strangely different would it be from a photograph of the same subject taken in July, more especially when, as now, the elections throw everything into confusion; and little Haultort gets so bewildered, that he encloses, by mistake, his address to his constituents to Wild Harrie, instead of his proposal to her, which he has forwarded to his local attorney for publication in the Liberal organ of that borough which is honoured by possessing him as a representative!

In these days when good taste requires that our affections should be as shallow as our convictions, we are puzzled, at a crisis like this, to know which we love most, our seats or our mistresses. There is a general disposition on the part of the lavender-gloved tribe to resent the extra wear and tear of mind suddenly imposed upon them this hot weather. Why should they unexpectedly be called away from the corners devoted to *tête-à-têtes*, to stand on hotel balconies, and stammer, in unintelligible language, their views upon Reform to crowds of free and independent electors? "For goodness' sake," says Larkington to Lady Veriphast, "give me some ideas; I've got to go and meet these wretched constituents of mine, and I had promised myself a much more agreeable occupation with you at Richmond. Couldn't you get Veriphast to go down? I should be delighted to retire in his favour; and with his abilities it is ridiculous his not being in Parliament."

"How absurdly you talk about my persuading Veriphast to do anything? the only person, as you know, who has any influence over him is Mrs Loveton," responds her ladyship, with a sigh—arising from dyspepsia.

"I have hit it;" and for a moment Larkington looks animated. "Squabbleton is close to the coast, and we will make a party, and I will take you all round in my yacht, the Lovetons and you and Veriphast; we'll go and do the electioneering business together, and keep the yacht as a sort of *pied à terre*, or rather *pied à mer*;" and Larkington chuckled, partly at his joke, and partly at this brilliant solution of his dilemma.

And so, while all the world is trying to reconcile their pleasure with what they are pleased to term their duty, being always the duty they owe to themselves, my thoughts are diverted into a very different channel. I am beginning daily to feel, while in the world, that I am less of it. Already I have cut myself off from the one great source of interest which Parliament afforded me, and I have not succeeded in my love as a compensation—that is why Larkington's arrangement to secure both seemed a sort of mockery of my misery. For it was impossible to resist the occasional fits of depression which reduced my mind to the condition of white paper, and the world to that of a doll stuffed with sawdust. I was suffering in this manner the day following the evening entertainment at Lady Broadhem's, which I have already described. The interview which impended inspired me with vague terrors. The night before I had looked forward to it with positive enjoyment. There is no greater bore than to get up morally and physically unhinged, upon the very day that you expect an unusual strain upon your faculties. The days it does not matter, you feel up to anything; but nature too often perversely deserts you at the most critical moment.

Now, upon the morning in question it was necessary as a preliminary measure for me to go into the City and acquire some information essential to the success of my interview with Lady Broadhem, but before starting I was anxious to gain a few particulars from Grandon, the knowledge of which would materially aid me in disentangling the complicated skein of our joint affairs. I therefore looked in upon him for a moment *en passant*.

"I went to Lady Broadhem's last night, Grandon," I said, "and I have reasons for wishing to know whether you have had any communication with the family lately. I think the time is coming when I shall be able to explain much of my conduct which I can well understand has perplexed and distressed you."

"It would be a relief to me to feel that there was no more mystery between us," he replied. "You have certainly at last most effectually contradicted the report you were the means of originating, but the reparation was tardy, and should never have been rendered necessary. However, there is no use in recurring to the past; but I am entitled to ask what your object is in making your present inquiries?"

"I am to see Lady Broadhem this afternoon," I said, "and I wish to be prepared on all points. I heard something last night which may influence your future far more seriously than mine; and it is in fact in your interests, and not in my own, that I wish to be well informed."

"What do you want to know?"

"I want to know whether you have ever actually proposed to Lady Ursula, and, if so, what was the result?"

"Frank," said Grandon, "after what has passed you are pushing my confidence in you, and my friendship for you, to their utmost limits, in expecting me to answer you in this matter. Still I cannot believe your motives to be unworthy, though they may be unintentionally perverted; nor do I think that it is in your power to affect the position of affairs either for good or harm. The fact is, then, that Lady Ursula does know precisely the state of my feelings towards her, and I feel that, though there may be insuperable obstacles to our union at present, she would never consent to yield to any pressure exercised by her mother in favour of another."

"In other words, the situation is unchanged, for I think I knew as much as that before. Have you never spoken to Lady Broadhem directly on the subject?"

"No," said Grandon—"never."

"I think," said I, "the time is coming when you will be able to do so with advantage. I cannot tell you more now, but this afternoon I shall hope to retrieve myself in your estimation by being the bearer of some good news. By the way, what are you going to do about your election?—they say your prospects are getting cloudy."

"Say rather utterly obscured," he replied. "You know the borough I sit for is in Lord Scilly's pocket, and he says I have not sufficiently stuck to my party. They have never forgiven me for understanding the Schleswig-Holstein question; and Scilly has extracted a promise from his new nominee that he is never to inform himself upon any question of foreign politics. The Government is so weak in this department that they are more afraid of their own *enfants terribles* than they are of the Opposition, which is not saying much for the latter."

"Who is Scilly's new nominee?" I asked.

"No less a person than our old friend Chundango," he replied. "It seems Lady Broadhem put pressure upon his lordship in his favour, and he at last consented, though I suspect it was with a bad grace."

"Well, I don't think the Government need be afraid of Chundango on foreign policy, though he probably knows as much as the others."

It required no little effort to reach Bodwinkle's office at 10 A.M. I found that great millionaire in a peculiarly amiable frame of mind. Though two or three of his neighbours had been smashing around him, his superior foresight had enabled him to escape the calamities which had overtaken them; and he was sitting chuckling in that rather dingy alley, from the recesses of which he had dug his fortune, when I entered.

"Ah, Lord Frank," he said, affably; "come to give me some of your valuable advice and assistance in my election affairs, I feel sure. Don't forget your promise about Stepton. I have already given the necessary instructions about that matter of Lady Broadhem's; there is nothing going to be done about it for the present."

"It is just with reference to Lady Broadhem's affairs that I have come to consult you," I said. "You have a pretty extensive Indian connection, I think?"

"Rather," said Bodwinkle, in a tone which meant to imply gigantic.

"Now I have reason to believe that her ladyship is interested in some Bombay houses, and I shall be able to throw some light upon her affairs which may be of use to us both, if you will give me the benefit of a little of that exclusive information with reference to cotton and those who are embarked in its trade which I know you possess."

Bodwinkle was loath at first to let me into those mysteries which he speedily revealed to me on my explaining more fully my reasons for requiring to know them, and I jumped into a hansom and drove off to Grosvenor Square, planning a little plot which I completed ere I arrived, and the construction of which had acted as beneficially upon my nerves as one of Lady Broadhem's own "pick-me-ups." Drippings let me in, and his countenance wore an expression of anxious consciousness. As he led the way up-stairs he whispered, "I trust, my lord, that under the circumstances your lordship will not betray me—my own livelihood, not to say that of my wife and little ones, depends upon my keeping this place; and I would not have mentioned what had come to my knowledge with respect to her ladyship if it had not been that, knowing the interest your lordship takes in the family, and more especially when I come to consider Lady Ursula——"

"Hold your tongue," I interrupted, angrily. "If you wish me to reduce you and your family to beggary, dare to open your lips to me again unless you're spoken to." I felt savage with him for ruffling my temper at the moment when I desired to have my faculties completely under control; and as my readers will have perceived, though my intentions are always excellent, my course is occasionally, under any unusual strain, erratic.

I never saw Lady Broadhem looking better. One or two wrinkles were positively missing altogether, and an expression of cheerful benevolence seemed to play about the corners of her mouth. She greeted me with an *empressement* totally at variance with the terms on which we had parted upon the previous evening. I must say that, when Lady Broadhem chooses, there is nobody of my acquaintance whose manner is more attractive, and whose conversation is more agreeable. She had been a *belle* in her day, and had achieved some renown among the "wholly-worldlies" when she first married the late lord. Her "history," connected chiefly with another lord of that period, is not yet altogether forgotten. The end of it was, that the world looked coldly upon her ladyship for a few seasons, and she scrambled with some difficulty into the society of the "worldly-holies," among whom she has ever since remained. There are occasions when a certain amount of coquetry of manner betrays the existence of some of those "devil's leavings" which she is still engaged in sacrificing. Had it not been for the information I had derived from Drippings, her cordial reception and unembarrassed manner would have puzzled me. As it was, I felt assured by the indications they furnished, that the butler had told me the truth.

"My dear Lady Broadhem," I said, with enthusiasm, "how well you are looking! I am sure you must have some charming news to tell me. Is some near and wealthy relation dead, or what?"

"For shame, Frank! what a satirical creature you are! Do you know I only discovered lately that irony was your strong point? I am positively beginning to be afraid of you."

"Come now," I said, "own frankly, what you have to tell me to-day makes you feel more afraid of me than you ever did before."

Lady Broadhem blushed—yes, actually blushed. It was not the flush of anger which I had often seen dye her cheeks, or of shame, which I never did; but it was a blush of maiden consciousness, if I may so express it, though it is occasionally to be observed in widows. It mounted slowly and suffused her whole neck and face, even unto the roots of her hair; it was a blush of that kind which I have seen technically described by a German philosopher as a "rhythm of exquisite sweetness."

The effect of this hardened old lady indulging in a rhythm of this description struck me as so ludicrous that I was compelled to resort to my pocket-handkerchief and pretend to sneeze behind it. At the same moment Lady Broadhem resorted to hers, and applied it with equal sincerity to her eyes. "Dear Frank," she said, and sobbed. "Dear Lady Broadhem," I responded, and nearly choked with suppressed laughter, for I knew what was coming.

"All my money difficulties are at an end at last, and if I am affected, it is that I feel I am not worthy of the happiness that is in store for me," and she lifted up her eyes, in which real tears were actually glistening, and said, "What have I done to deserve it?"

"Well, really," I replied, "if you ask me that question honestly, I must wait till I know what 'it' is; perhaps you would have been better without—'it.'"

"I assure you, Frank, one of the uppermost feelings in my mind is that of relief. I fully appreciate the warm-hearted generosity which has prompted you to take so much interest in my affairs; but when it was all over between you and Ursula, my conscience would not allow me to let you make pecuniary sacrifices on so large a scale for my sake. When Broadhem told me that you had determined to persevere in your munificence, notwithstanding Ursula's most inexplicable conduct, I made up my mind at once to adopt a course which, I am happy to say, not merely my sense of propriety but my feelings told me was the right one. I must therefore relieve you from all further anxiety about my business matters. You have, I think, still got some papers of mine, which you may return to me; and I will see that my solicitor not only releases you from any engagements which you may have entered into for me, but will repay those sums which you have so kindly advanced on my account already."

There was a tone of triumph pervading this speech which clearly meant, "Now we are quits. I don't forget the time when you drank my 'pick-me-up' first, and biologised me afterwards. And this is my revenge."

I must say I looked at Lady Broadhem with a certain feeling of admiration. She was a woman made up of "forces." Last night passionate and intemperate under the influence of the society she had called round her: to-day calm and wily, using her advantages of situation with a judgment and a moderation worthy of a great strategist. She is only arrogant and insolent in the hour of disaster; but she can conquer magnanimously. I assumed an air of the deepest regret and disappointment. "Of course, Lady Broadhem, any change in your circumstances which makes you independent, even of your friends, must be agreeable to you; but I cannot say how deeply disappointed I feel that my labour of love is over, and that I shall no longer have the pleasure of spending my resources in a cause so precious to me." The last words almost stuck in my throat; but I wanted to overdo it, to see the effect.

"My dear Frank," she said, laughing, and her eyes would have twinkled had they not become too watery from age, "I shall never make you out; I am so stupid at reading character, and I suppose so dull altogether, that sometimes I am not sure when you're joking and when you are in earnest. Now I want you seriously to answer me truly one question, not as people of the world, you know, making pledges to each other, but as old friends, as we are, who may dispense with mystery." She held out her hand with an air of charming candour. "Tell me," she said, as she pressed mine,—"tell me honestly, what could possibly have been your motive in being prepared to go on sacrificing your fortune for me when you had no chance of Ursula?"

"Tell me honestly, Lady Broadhem," I said, and pressed her hand in return, "how you are going to render yourself independent of my assistance hence-forward, and I will tell you the motives which have actuated me in proffering it."

"It is only just settled, and I have not even told it yet either to Broadhem or my daughters. I am quite prepared for the sensation it will make when it is known, and the ill-natured things people will say of me; but my mind is made up, and we are told to expect persecution. I am going to be married to Mr Chundango!"

Lady Broadhem evidently expected to stun me with this announcement, but as I had already been prepared for it by Drippings on the occasion of our first private interview, which the reader will remember, I received it with perfect equanimity.

"I had no conception," her ladyship went on, "of the sterling worth and noble character of that man until I had an opportunity of observing it closely. The munificence of his liberality, and the good uses to which he applies his enormous wealth, the cultivation of his mind, the excellence of his principles, and the perfect harmony of feeling upon religious subjects which exists between us, all convince me that I shall best consult my own happiness and the interests of my dear children by uniting my fate to his. I suppose you know Lord Scilly is going to put him into Parliament for the Scilly boroughs instead of Lord Grandon?"

"No one could congratulate you more sincerely than I do, Lady Broadhem," I said. "I can conceive no greater happiness than an alliance in which that perfect harmony of thought and feeling you describe reigns paramount; and now it is my turn to tell you why I have acted the part which seems so incomprehensible to you. Grandon is, as you know, my dearest friend, but he is poor. Ursula cares for him more, if possible, than I do. And I need not tell you that my own attachment to your daughter is the strongest sentiment of my nature. Now, I determined to prove the depth of my affection for these two people by making them both happy, and when all my arrangements were completed I intended to make a final stipulation with you, that you should give your consent to their marriage, and that I should play the part of a bountiful prince in the Arabian Nights, and that we should all live happy ever after."

"A very pretty little plot indeed," said Lady Broadhem, with a sneer. "You are too good and disinterested for this planet, Frank. So you thought you could coerce me into giving my consent to a marriage I never have approved, and never shall?"

"Don't be too sure of that," I said, and I allowed the faintest tinge of insolence to appear in my manner, for the sentiments and the sneer that accompanied it both irritated me, and I felt that we were morally drawing our revolvers, and looking at the caps.

"Why not? What do you mean?" she said, sharply. "Who do you suppose is to dictate to me upon such a subject? Ursula will be very well off, and I shall take care that she marries suitably."

"I don't know where she is to get her money from," I said, calmly.

"You need give yourself no anxiety about her for the future, I assure you. Mr Chundango has been most liberal in his arrangements about both my girls."

"But, unfortunately, it is not in Mr Chundango's power to make any such arrangements," I retorted. "I am sure nothing will alter your feelings towards a man you really love, and that your own personal conduct will not be influenced by the fact that Mr Chundango is a beggar. You could go back to India with him, you know, and make a home for him in a bungalow in the Bombay Ghauts."

Lady Broadhem's face had become rigid and stony; so had my whole nature. I did not feel a particle of compassion or of triumph. I was cold, hard, and judicial. Her hour was come, and I had to pass the sentence. "Yes," I said, "there is no doubt about it. I got it from Bodwinkle this moment. The Bombay mail arrived last night, and you know the way everything has been crashing there through speculations in Back Bay shares, cotton, &c. Well, the great Parsee house of Burstupjee Cockabhoy has come down with a grand crash, and all our friend Chundango's jewels in the back verandah, added to everything else he possesses in the world, will fail to meet his liabilities. Terrible thing, isn't it? but we must bear up, you know."

But Lady Broadhem had done bearing up some time ago, and had sunk gently back on the couch, in a dead faint. As there was not the slightest sham about it, I rang the bell for Jenkins, and felt under the pillow for the "pick-me-up," which I failed to make her swallow; so I slapped the soles of her feet with her shoes, till her maid arrived, followed by Drippings, who, I suspect, had spent some portion of his time in the neighbourhood of the keyhole.

"I will go and look for Lady Ursula," I said; "where shall I find her?"

"In her own 'boudwore,'" said Jenkins—"first door on the right, at the top of the stairs," and I left Lady Broadhem being ministered to with sal-volatile, and went in search of her daughter.

Lady Ursula was writing, and as she looked up I saw the traces of tears upon her cheeks, though she smiled as she frankly gave me her hand. "I half expected you, Lord Frank, as I knew you were to call on mamma to-day, and I thought you would not leave without seeing me; but I expected to have been sent for. Don't you know that this is very sacred ground, and that the privilege of treading upon it is accorded to very few?"

"I have that to tell you," I said, gravely, "which I can only talk of privately. I have left Lady Broadhem downstairs, and it is the result of my interview with her that I want to communicate to you. Do you know that she contemplated taking a very serious step?"

I did not know how to approach the subject, and felt embarrassed now that I found myself obliged to explain to a daughter that her mother was going to marry the man that daughter had rejected, as an act of revenge.

"No," said Lady Ursula. "I have suspected by her preoccupied manner for many days past that mamma had decided upon something, but I have shrunk from speaking to her of her own plans. Indeed she seemed to have avoided me in a way which she never did before."

"Before telling you what she intended doing, I must premise that she has quite abandoned the idea; therefore don't let yourself be distressed by what might have been, but won't be now."

I risked this assertion as, though Lady Broadhem had not told me that she had abandoned the idea, and was at that moment in a dead faint, I felt certain that her first impulse on "coming to" would be to abandon it. "Well," said Lady Ursula, with her lip trembling and her eye cast down, "if you think it right that you should tell me, do so; remember she is my mother."

"It was nothing so very dreadful after all," I said, and tried to reassure her by a careless manner—for I saw how much she dreaded the unknown.

"The fact is, Lady Broadhem has been driven to despair by the family embarrassments, and we must make allowances for her under the circumstances. Then perhaps she was under the influence of pique. At all events, she has made up her mind to accept a proposal which Mr Chundango had the audacity to make."

Lady Ursula raised her eyes in a bewildered way to mine. It was evident that she had failed even now to comprehend me. What business, I thought, had I to come up here after all? It is a piece of impertinence in me; and I trembled at my rashness. What will she think? I shall shock her, and ruin myself in her estimation irretrievably; and I wished myself back again, slapping the soles of Lady Broadhem's feet; but Lady Broadhem was already making use of those very soles, and was marching up-stairs at that identical moment; for before I could find words to explain my meaning more fully to Lady Ursula, and while I was yet doubting whether I should not back out of the whole subject, in stalked her ladyship, very white, with lips compressed, and an expression on her face which so terrified Ursula that she forgot my speech in the amazement and alarm which her mother's aspect caused her. "What are you doing in my daughter's private sitting-room, Lord Frank?" said Lady Broadhem, between her teeth.

"I came to tell her of your sudden illness, and explain the cause of it," I replied, calmly.

"And have you done so?" and I saw how much depended on my answer by the nervous way in which Lady Broadhem clenched her hand to control her emotion: she has given me a good many *mauvais quarts d'heures*, I thought—I will give her one now.

"I was just telling Lady Ursula," I said, "that Mr Chundango had positively had the impudence to propose to you"—Lady Broadhem gave a sort of suppressed scream—"when you came in."

"Then you did not tell her what he proposed?" she said.

"No, I leave that to you," I said, maliciously.

"My dear Ursula, I would not tell you, because I know you do not approve of speculations, and I feel myself that they are questionable, if not actually sinful. My dear child, I did it for the best; Chundango wanted me to join him in one of his Indian speculations, and proposed to me to"—Lady Broadhem paused, coloured, looked me full in the face, and then said slowly—"to unite my resources to his. Fortunately, Lord Frank has just discovered in time that he is a bankrupt, so of course all partnership arrangements between us are at an end, and I am most thankful for the lesson. You know I promised you once before that I would give up trying to retrieve my own fortunes by commercial speculation, even of the most legitimate description; and now, my dear Frank, and you, my sweet child, forgive me for having even thought of yielding to this temptation. You must have seen how much it has weighed upon me, Ursula dear, for some time past; but let us be thankful that I have been saved from it," and the handkerchief was again called into requisition.

Well done, Lady Broadhem! that was a triumph of white-lying, and the best piece of acting you have done in my presence; it so touched Lady Ursula that she threw herself on her mother's neck.

"Never mind, mamma; I know that whatever you do is out of love for us; but indeed we don't want to be rich. Broadhem has no expensive tastes, and I would only be too glad to get away from London. Let us let the house, and take a little cottage somewhere in the country,—we shall be so much happier;" and Lady Ursula nestled herself on her mother's cheek, little dreaming that she had nearly had Chundango for a father-in-law, and evidently much relieved at finding that this dreadful intelligence, for which I was preparing her, was not some horrid crime, but only another money affair. As I looked at the mother and daughter, clasped in each other's arms, and pictured to myself the thoughts that were hidden in those hearts now palpitating against each other, I felt that it would almost be a righteous act to tear them asunder for ever.

Never mind, you have given me a hold over you that I shall turn to account; that lie was dexterously worded, and evidenced infinite presence of mind; but you will have first to throw over Chundango, and then to shut his mouth, and then you will have to shut mine, and finally to shut Drippings his mouth. Oh, my dear Lady Broadhem, what a very slimy and disagreeable course you have marked out for yourself!

"Mr Chundango is in the drawing-room, my lady," said Drippings, appearing at the door at this critical juncture; and he took a survey of the group as one who should say within himself, "Here is some new start which I am not yet up to, but which I soon shall be," and he waited at the door to observe the effect of his intelligence.

"I shall be down immediately," said Lady Broadhem, coldly; and Drippings vanished. "Perhaps, under the circumstances, you had better leave Mr Chundango to my tender mercies," I said, significantly. "There can be no reason why you should *ever* see him again." I emphasised the word "ever" purposely, and assumed a tone of authority under which Lady Broadhem winced. Our eyes met for a moment, and then I looked at her nose, and I am sure she read my thought, which was "I must keep it on the grindstone," for she sighed and acquiesced.

"How do, my dear Mr Chundango?" said I, gaily, to the Oriental, who seemed rather taken aback when he saw me enter the drawing-room instead of Lady Broadhem, and whose lips got paler than was altogether consistent with their usual colour. "I must congratulate you on the prospect of becoming a legislator. I hear Lord Scilly is going to put you in for his boroughs."

"Yes," said Chundango, affectedly. "His lordship has been good enough to press them upon me, but I have determined not to go in as any man's nominee. The fact is, I wanted to ask Lady Broadhem's advice upon that very matter, and have come here expressly to do so."

"She is not very well, and has deputed me to consult with you instead. Come," I said, confidentially. "What is it all about? I shall be too glad to assist you."

The puzzled expression of Chundango's face at this moment was a study: "Has Lady Broadhem told him everything or not?—How much does he know?—What line shall I take?" and he stroked his chin doubtfully.

"Come, out with it," I said, sharply; "I haven't time to stand here all day waiting till you decide how much you will tell me and how much you won't." Now this is the kind of speech which disturbs a native more than any other, but which would be inexcusable in polite society. I had lived too much in the East to be trammelled with the conventionalities of Europe, and my friend felt as much, for he cringed at once after the manner of his race.

"I have no intention of deceiving you," he said. "I don't know whether Lady Broadhem has told you that we are to be united in matrimony?"

"Yes," I said, "she has."

"Well, I want to make arrangements by which the ceremony may be accomplished without delay, for I feel the suspense is trying. Might I ask you to find out the earliest moment which would suit her convenience? I need not say that I hope you will be present."

"I suppose you would prefer it, if possible, before the arrival of the next mail from Bombay?" I said.

Chundango, who is by no means deficient in intelligence, saw at a glance that it was useless to attempt to deceive me. "I see that you know," he said, meekly, "the terrible misfortune by which I have been overtaken, through no fault of my own. I am quite sure it will not affect Lady Broadhem's resolution."

"I am quite sure it will," I said; "and the fact is, as she did not want a scene, she sent me down to give you to understand that everything is at an end between you. You look surprised," I went on, for Chundango was not yet so familiar with the customs of polite society, as to believe such heartless conduct on the part of Lady Broadhem possible; "but I assure you this is the usual form among ladies in London. I am well aware no Hindoo woman would have done it; but you must remember, Mr Chundango, that you are in a Christian and a civilised country, where money is essential to make the pot boil—not in a tropical heathen land where a pocket-handkerchief is sufficient for clothing, and a few plantains for sustenance. We don't keep our hearts in a state of nature in this country a bit more than our bodies—it would not be considered proper; you'll soon get over it"—but Chundango's eyes were gleaming with revenge.

"Ah!" he said, drawing his breath with a sibilant sound, "everybody in London shall hear how I have got over it."

"Nobody would believe you, and you would only be laughed at. Lady Broadhem would flatly deny it. We always do deny those little episodes. My good innocent Chundango, how much you have to learn, and how simple and guileless they are in your native country to what we are here! No, no! come with me; I will do the best for everybody, and send you back to your mother dutiful and repentant—you had no business ever to desert her;" and I rang the bell.

"Tell Lady Broadhem," I said to Drippings, "that I have gone with Mr Chundango into the City, and will call again to-morrow." I took Chundango straight to Bodwinkle's, and found the millionaire in close confabulation with Spiffy Goldtip. Between them was the address to the electors of Shuffleborough, with which my readers are already familiar.

"We must alter it slightly," said Spiffy as I entered.

"What! haven't you issued it yet?" I asked.

"No," he said; "we were just going to send it out to-day."

"Then I am in time to stop you. Your address, Spiffy, so outraged Stepton, that he has determined to stand himself, and neither you nor Bodwinkle have a chance; so I would advise you to keep that document back," I said, turning to Bodwinkle, who looked dumbfounded and crestfallen.

"A nice mess you have got me into between you," he said, sulkily gazing at us both.

"Spiffy has, but my turn has yet to come. Bodwinkle, I think you know more of Mr Chundango's affairs than any one else; in fact, I suppose you have what the tradesmen call 'a little account' between you. He wishes to say a few words confidentially to you, while I want to have a moment alone with Spiffy."

"You know all about him?" I said, nodding towards Chundango.

"Collapsed, hasn't he?" said Spiffy.

"Yes," I said, "but it won't be known for a day or two. At present he is Lord Scilly's nominee. Bodwinkle wants a borough. He may either ignore his last programme, as it is not yet issued, and adopt Scilly's political views, or, if he is too conscientious, when Chundango retires at the last moment, he may snatch the seat. All that is your affair—you know Scilly and Bodwinkle both better than I do. Now I have reasons for wanting Chundango shipped back at once to Bombay, and for wishing to close this long-standing affair of Lady Broadhem's with Bodwinkle. Make the best terms you can for Chundango, and see what Bodwinkle is disposed to do in the other matter; and let me know the result to-morrow. Keep Chundango here now to refer to. Good-bye, Bodwinkle," I called out; "Spiffy has got some good news to give you, but be merciful to our friend here," and I passed my arm through Chundango's and drew him to a corner. "Now, look here," I said, in a whisper, "if you will bury the recollection of what has passed between you and Lady Broadhem, and never breathe a word of it even in your dreams, I will get Bodwinkle to start you again in Bombay, but you must go back at once and stay there. Now you may stay here, for you will be wanted." I saw Spiffy meantime imparting to Bodwinkle his projects for turning to account the new prospects I had been the means of opening out to him.

"Dear me," I thought, as I for the second time that day threaded my way westwards from the City, "all this is unravelling itself very neatly, considering how much dirt is mixed up in it, but it is not quite far enough advanced to be communicated to Grandon." The fact is, I had a sort of suspicion that he would not altogether approve of my mode of carrying my point, even when my only desire was to secure his and Ursula's happiness. No, I thought; he would have scruples, and object, and bother. I won't tell him anything till it is all done; but I must tell him something, as I promised him some good news to-day, and he is waiting at home on purpose.

"Well, old fellow, I think I have got a borough for you, after all. It stupidly did not occur to me before, but you are just the man for the constituency."

"I thought you had been to Lady Broadhem's, and were to bring me back some good news," said Grandon, with a disappointed air.

"So I have," I replied, "but I am bound to secrecy for another twenty-four hours; meantime, listen! I am going to retire from Dunderhead. I wrote my address a few days ago, but did not send it. They are therefore quite unprepared. I will retire to-morrow; the nomination is to be in two or three days; and what with the suddenness of the affair and my influence, your return is certain."

"You going to retire!" said Grandon, astounded. "Why, you never told me of this. When did you make up your mind?"

"It made itself up, as it always does," I said, laughing. "It never puts me in the painful position of having to decide, but takes its own line at once. I am going to America by the next steamer." Now, when I tell my readers that when I began to talk to Grandon I had no intention whatever of going to America, they will be able to form some idea, if they have not done so already, of what a funny mind mine is. It came upon me with the irresistible force of an inspiration, and from that moment I was morally booked and bound at all hazards to go.

Grandon knew me so well that he was less surprised than he might have been, and only sighed deeply. He felt at that moment that there was something hopelessly wrong about me. He had been so often encouraged by a certain steadiness which I maintained for some time, and which led him to think me changed, and so often disappointed; for when he least expected it I broke the slender fetters of common-sense and conventionalism, which he and society between them had woven round me, and went off at a tangent.

"Never mind, old fellow," I said, laughing, "there is no use sighing over me. I have pleasures and satisfactions arising from within that I should not have if I was like everybody else. Now, for instance:"—and the eagerness and turmoil which my new project excited within me seemed to reduce every other consideration to insignificance, for I began to feel conscious that, somehow or other, though I had often been in America before, this time it was to be to me a newer world than ever.

"Are you going alone?" said Grandon; for I had not finished my sentence.

"No," I said; and I guessed who my companion was to be, though no words had been exchanged between us.

"Who IS going with you?" he asked, wonderingly, for my manner struck him, and I scarcely heard his question, so wrapt at that instance seemed all my faculties. I think I fell asleep and dreamt, but I can't recall exactly what I seemed to see. Grandon was shaking me, I thought, in the most heartless manner, and I told him as much when I opened my eyes. The fact was, I was a little knocked up with excitement; but I would not go and lie down till he promised me to stand for Dunderhead. Then I went to bed, and did not get up till the lamps were being lighted in Piccadilly.

The result of such irregular hours was that I was in bed next morning when Spiffy Goldtip knocked at my bedroom-door. He had worked very hard in Lady Broadhem's interest, and explained to me the scheme which he had arranged with Bodwinkle, by means of which, at a very considerable sacrifice of my own capital, I could start Lady Broadhem and her son afresh in the world, on a very limited income, but devoid of encumbrances of a threatening or embarrassing nature. I would far rather have invested the same amount in securing a larger income to Grandon and Ursula, if they were ever destined to be united; but I knew that, in the first place, nothing would induce them to take it from me; and in the second, that I could only even now hope to extort Lady Broadhem's consent to the match by the prospect I was enabled to hold out to her of a period of financial repose. After all, my own wants were moderate, and £15,000 a-year satisfied them as well as £20,000.

"We accomplished great things yesterday," said Spiffy, rubbing his hands gleefully, for he had himself benefited by the settlement above alluded to. "When I showed Bodwinkle that we could make the Scilly boroughs a certainty, he behaved like a gentleman, and our friend Chundango is to go out to Bombay by the next mail, under more favourable conditions than he could have possibly expected. Of course I shall retire from contesting Shuffleborough to the more congenial atmosphere of Homburg. Heigho!" sighed Spiffy, "I have gone through a good deal of wear and tear this season, and want to recruit."

I got rid of Spiffy as soon as I had heard what he had to say, and I was so satisfied with his intelligence that I determined at once to see Grandon, and to take him with me to Lady Broadhem's. "Grandon," I said, abruptly entering his room, "I want you to come with me at once to Grosvenor Square."

"Did Lady Broadhem tell you to ask me?" He looked up with such a sad, wistful gaze as he said this, that my heart melted towards him, for I felt I had spoken roughly; so I drew a chair close to him, and, sitting by his side, placed my arm in his as we did in the old school-days.

"My dear old fellow, the moment is come for you to prove your friendship by trusting me thoroughly. I know how rudely Lady Broadhem has always behaved to you whenever you have met—I know how my conduct has perplexed and grieved you. Well, now, I have come to ask you to forgive us both."

"I have nothing to forgive; but it would be an utter want of taste in me to go there unless she expects me, and wishes to see me, and I can hardly hope that," he said, with a forced smile.

For a moment I doubted whether I dared to risk it, but I had placed Lady Broadhem in a position upon which I could venture a good deal, and I longed for the triumph and gratification of enjoying the success of my own handiwork. It would be a triumph full of alloy, but I wanted to see how much I could achieve and—bear; so my hesitation vanished.

"I will take the responsibility on myself," I said; "and believe me, I would not urge it if I was not perfectly certain that I was doing what is right. Remember how many times I have blindly followed your advice. I only ask you this once to follow mine, and secure your own happiness."

The temptation was too strong, and Grandon yielded; but it was with a reluctant, doubtful step that he approached the door he had not this year ventured to enter. It was opened by Drippings, and I took the opportunity of having a little private conversation with him in the hall, in the course of which it was arranged that he should exchange her ladyship's service for mine, and accompany me to America: the truth is, I proposed settling him there, and making him send for his wife and family. He knew too much of Lady Broadhem's affairs to be at all a desirable domestic either to herself or to her friends in this country.

"Lady Broadhem is in her own sitting-room, my lord," said Drippings; "shall I show your lordship up to her?"

"No; if there is nobody in the drawing-room, take us there first. Now, Grandon, I will send for you when you are wanted; keep quiet, and don't get impatient;" and I left him and knocked at Lady Broadhem's door.

The events of the last twenty-four hours had told upon her, and the old wrinkles had come back, with several new ones. She was at that critical age when a great grief or anxiety can make an elderly person antiquated in a night—just as hair will turn grey in a few hours. She put out her hand without speaking, but with an expression of resignation which seemed to say, "I acknowledge myself beaten; be a brute or anything else you like; trample upon me, pray—I am down without the possibility of retaliating, but you will get very little sport out of me; badger me if you like, I don't mean to show fight." All this I read in her face as plainly as if she had said it; and I thought this a moment when generosity on the part of the victor will prove one to be a true strategist; and no one will appreciate it more than Lady Broadhem. With great gentleness, and without allowing a shade of self-satisfaction to cross my face or to penetrate my tones, I told her how I had propitiated Bodwinkle, banished Chundango, provided for Drippings, and succeeded at last in placing her affairs generally on a sound footing.

"Your genius will never be appreciated by the world, Frank," she said, smiling half ironically, half sadly.

"I am quite aware of that," I replied; "nor will this record of my experiences in it—except by you and one or two others who know how true it is. And now, Lady Broadhem, you know the wish which is nearest my heart, but which I don't venture to put in words,"—and I held out my hand.

"Yes," she said—and I saw the slender nostril dilate with the effort it cost her to yield the point upon which she had been so long inflexible—"you want my consent to Ursula's marriage with Grandon. I give it."

"Wait a minute; I should like Lady Ursula to be present," I said; for even now I did not feel that I could trust the old lady thoroughly, and I rang the bell. It was delightful to see how submissively Lady Broadhem sent for Lady Ursula, and how kindly she greeted both son and daughter as they entered, for Broadhem accompanied his sister.

"I have sent for you, my dear," she said, "to tell you how much we owe to our kind friend here, who has completely relieved my mind from all those anxieties which have been weighing upon it for the last few years, by his noble and generous conduct. Ursula, dear, you will never know really how much you owe him, for he has shown me that I have not done my duty to you as a mother;" and Lady Broadhem's voice trembled. "Upon my word," I thought, "I do believe the old woman is sincere;" and I looked at her fixedly. The tears were filling her eyes. Now pray heaven that we have got to heart at last—it is like sinking a well in a thirsty desert, and coming on water. Yes, there they are welling out, honest large drops, chasing each other to the point of her nose. Oh, my dear Lady Broadhem, I am beginning to love you, and my eyes are beginning to swim too; and before she knew where she was, I threw my arms round her neck and kissed her—an example which was rapidly followed both by Ursula and Broadhem, and which so overcame their mother that she buried her face in a pillow and sobbed out—in tears that might at first have been bitter, but were assuredly sweet and refreshing at last—her repentance. I don't think Broadhem had any very definite idea why he wept, beyond a feeling of sympathy with his mother, and the fact, which I afterwards heard, that Wild Harrie had taken Spiffy's advice, and refused him; so he mingled his tears with hers, but Lady Ursula's eyes were dry and supernaturally brilliant. As I gazed on the group, my own heart seemed to swell to bursting. I do really believe and trust that Lady Broadhem will give up the worldly-holies, and become a pious good woman; and that those talents and that force of character which she possesses may be dedicated to a higher service than they have heretofore been. If I have been the humble instrument of working the change, the sooner I send Grandon here and vanish myself from the scene, the better, or I shall become vain and conceited, I thought; and I rose from my seat.

"Good-bye, Lady Broadhem," I said, "you will not see me again. I am going to America in three days, and must go to Flityville to-morrow; but I never thought I could have bid you all farewell and felt so happy at the prospect of parting;" and I threw one yearning glance on Ursula in spite of myself. "Your happiness is secured, I do most firmly believe," I said to her; "and as for you," and I laid my hand on Broadhem's shoulder, "remember the experiment I proposed to you the other night, and try it;" and I was moving off when Ursula seized my hand, and almost dragged me back to her mother's side. She lifted up her eyes like one inspired, and the radiancy of her expression seemed to dazzle and blind me. Then she knelt down, and I knelt by her side, while her mother lay before us, her whole frame heaving with convulsive sobs, and Broadhem stood by wondering and awestruck. I can't repeat that prayer here, but there was a power in those gentle accents which stilled the stormy elements, as the waves of the sea were once stilled before; and when the thrilling voice ceased there was a great calm, and we knew that a change had been affected in that place. Then the floodgates were opened which had been to that moment barred, and Lady Ursula threw herself on her mother's bosom, and wept tears of gratitude, and I stole silently away to the drawing-room, and led Grandon by the hand, without uttering a word, to that room into which a new atmosphere had descended, and a new breath had called into existence a new nature. He started back on the threshold at the picture before him. Lady Broadhem, apparently scarcely conscious, clasped in the arms of her weeping daughter; and Broadhem— poor Broadhem—bewildered at the sight of the strong woman he had dreaded and worshipped thus suddenly breaking down, was sitting on a footstool at his mother's side, holding one of her hands, helplessly.

"Good God! Frank," said Grandon, in a whisper, for neither Lady Broadhem nor her daughter saw us, "what have you been doing?"

"Beginning the work which is left for you to finish;" and I gently disengaged one of Lady Ursula's hands, and drew it towards me. "On you," I said to her solemnly, "has been bestowed a great gift; use it as you have done, and may he share it with you, and support you in the lifelong trial it must involve, and in the ridicule to which you will both be exposed. For myself, I go to seek it where I am told I shall alone find it." I placed her hand in Grandon's, kissed her mother on the forehead, and hurried from the room. Then the strain on my nervous system suddenly relaxed. I am conscious of Drippings helping me into a cab, and going with me to Piccadilly, and of one coming in and finding me stretched on my bed, and of his lifting me from it by a single touch, just as Drippings was going off in quest of the doctor. It was he who had met me that night when I was walking with Broadhem, but his name I am unable to divulge. "Stay here, my friend," he said to Drippings, "and pack your master's things: there is no need for the doctor; I will take him to America." And my heart leaped within me, for its predictions were verified, and the path lay clear before me.

And now, on this last night in England, as I pen the last lines of this record of my life during the six months that are past, and look back to the spirit in which it was begun, and examine the influences which impelled me to write as I have, I see that I too have undergone a change, and that the time has come when, if I wished, I can no more descant as heretofore on the faults and foibles of the day. Among those who have read me there may be some who have so well understood, that they will see why this is so. If in what I have said I have hurt the feelings of any man or woman in my desire to expose the vices of society at large, they will be of those who have failed to detect why I have said thus much, and needs must stop here; but none the less earnestly would I assure them that it has been against my will and intention to wound any one. As I began because I could not help it, so I end because I am obliged. My task is done. The seed which I found in my hand, such as it was, I have sown. Whether it rots and dies in the ground, or springs up and brings forth fruit, is a matter in which I cannot, and ought not, to have the smallest personal interest.

THE END.

[1] "Let the Church," says the 'Times,' in a recent leading article, "increase the number of her good things, and her ranks will be largely and *worthily* filled up."

[2] 'The Great Republic: a Poem of the Sun.' By Thomas Lake Harris. New York and London: published by the "The Brotherhood of the New Life."

Printed in Great Britain
by Amazon